BREAKING UP WITH NICENESS

A BOLD GIRLS' GUIDE TO GENUINE SELF-CARE

Discover the Power of Boundaries, Boldness, and Saying 'No'

SARAH BARRY

Published by
Storylane Books
hello@storylanebooks.com
www.storylanebooks.com

TABLE OF CONTENTS

Introduction: The Niceness Trap

Are you tired of constantly putting others before yourself? Are you fed up with smiling through discomfort and swallowing your true feelings? It's time to break free from the suffocating grip of niceness and step into your authentic power. Welcome to your bold girl's guide to genuine self-care.

Let me paint a picture that might hit close to home. Imagine yourself on a dance floor, dressed to the nines, feeling like a goddess in your own skin. But instead of owning the night on your terms, you find yourself trapped in a cycle of people-pleasing. You entertain conversations that drain your energy, tolerate touches that cross your boundaries, and plaster on a smile even when your soul is screaming *No*.

Sound familiar? That is the insidious grip of the "nice girl syndrome." It's that subtle yet suffocating pressure to prioritize others' comfort over your own, to smile through discomfort, and to never rock the boat. I lived this life for far too many years. The former people-pleaser in me couldn't help herself.

The nice girl syndrome causes exceptionally talented, stunning, strong, and beautiful women to tolerate situations simply because they feel compelled to maintain a pleasant demeanor—just to be nice!

Are you scratching your head wondering if you have fallen into the nice girl syndrome? Have you ever:

- Have you had trouble saying *no* or felt terrified to say it?

- Have you associated being loved with being nice?

- Have you found yourself struggling to establish boundaries?

- Have you found yourself taking feedback as rejection?

- Have you felt yourself forcing smiles to make others feel comfortable?

If you resonated with any or all of these, welcome to the nice girl club: a place most women reside.

From an early age, girls are taught to be kind and polite. When they behave nicely, they receive praise and positive feedback. This teaches young girls what behavior is considered appropriate in society. If you are kind and polite, your parents might praise you, or your teachers may say how nice you are. However, if you question things or show signs of rebellion, you are often corrected. You are told, "That isn't nice." Often, this pattern is passed down from mothers to daughters as a learned way of behaving.

But let me tell you something—being nice all the time is not a virtue; it's a burden. It dims your light, stifles your voice, and keeps you trapped in a cycle of self-doubt and resentment.

Does this behavior apply only to women? Being kind all the time is mostly a challenge for women but, on occasion, for men too. Though women are taught to be kind from early on, men don't generally receive the same upbringing.

Most Americans, especially women, make significant efforts to avoid conflict, and prioritize being nice. A higher percentage of women, 68% versus 61% of men, tend to prioritize others' needs over their own (Ballard, 2022).

But here's the good news: *You* hold the key to your freedom. In this book, we're diving deep into the tangled roots of nice girl syndrome and ripping them out once and for all. We'll unravel the myths that keep you shackled to people-pleasing, reclaim your right to set boundaries to say *no*, and speak your truth with unapologetic confidence.

Within these pages, you can expect to:

- Discover an understanding of why always pleasing others can be harmful to yourself.

- Uncover the importance of self-care, authentic living, and knowing your boundaries.

- Find exercises and activities to build confidence, discover communication skills, and uncover a solid plan on how this can be achieved in your daily life.

So, are you ready to rewrite the narrative of your life and reclaim your voice, your power, and your unapologetic authenticity? If so, get ready to embark on the most empowering chapter of your life. Together, we'll shatter the chains of niceness and unleash the bold, fearless warrior within you.

1

The Roots of Niceness

It is time to examine the undercurrents of niceness, unpack its origins, and shine a spotlight on its influence in our lives. Welcome to the exploration of the roots of niceness.

From the time we're little, we are taught the importance of being nice. "Be polite." "Say hello and smile." These mantras echo through our upbringing—a source of societal expectation and cultural norms. But what happens when niceness morphs from a virtue into a cage?

In this chapter, we are starting down a path back to the beginning, tracing the history of niceness through our lives. We'll unravel how society, family dynamics, and personal experiences have brought us together to create nice girl syndrome.

As we uncover these roots, we will discover the power of awareness—a key step to freedom. Armed with knowledge, we pave the way for transformation, shedding the layers of societal conditioning to reveal the authentic, courageous, and bold spirit within.

Ask yourself: *Are you ready to peel back the layers of niceness, and pave the way for a more authentic and empowered existence?*

The Origins of Nice Girl Syndrome

Think back through history and across different cultures. Women have been told repeatedly that being polite, nurturing, and accommodating is just part and parcel of being a woman. It's like society handed us this script where our role was to always put others' needs before our own, and to smile and nod even when we're seething inside.

You know those stories we grew up with, where the princesses were always sweet, gentle, and oh-so-nice? Cinderella took care of everyone in the castle, and Snow White took care of the dwarfs, and so on. They were like poster children for politeness—always striving to please others, even at their own expense.

And let's not forget those social norms that have been drilled into us since day one. We've been taught that being agreeable and bending over backward for others is the way to win love and acceptance. It's like being nice became our ticket to fitting in and being considered "good girls." How often were you told, or did you hear, "Don't be confrontational; it will only cause you problems"? We were conditioned to blend into the background and smile.

But somewhere along the way, being nice got twisted into something less empowering and more suffocating. It turned into this pressure cooker of expectations, where saying *no* felt like a cardinal sin and setting boundaries seemed downright rebellious.

We've been fed this idea that being anything other than nice—assertive, bold, real—somehow goes against the grain of femininity. While there is plenty of room to maintain politeness and nurturing qualities, it's also essential to recognize that being overly nice is not a requirement. Unfortunately, these concepts often become tangled, leading women to feel guilty for being true to themselves.

Cultural and Historical Perspectives

Throughout history, women were often pushed into second-class status. Think about it: In different parts of the world, girls were often denied the same education opportunities as boys. They were shut out from professions or roles that offered power or money. Even the money they earned often ended up in their husbands' pockets after marriage. Women had limited legal rights and did not have the right to vote. It's no wonder that social expectations demanded women to be passive, gentle, and solely valued for their appearance rather than their actions.

We have to be mindful that times have shifted. Feminism and social movements have paved the way for increased equality and changed these expectations. There's a growing interest in social history, shedding light on women's experiences and working-class struggles. Institutions are waking up to the need for diverse narratives, recognizing the importance of telling stories from multiple perspectives.

Now, let's talk about how this history translates into our daily lives. From a young age, we're told to "ask nicely" and "be nice," learning that expressing our own needs honestly is somehow rude. It's a script we've internalized, leading us to soften our speech, even phrasing statements as questions to avoid coming off as too assertive.

And let's not forget the tone policing. Women's voices are scrutinized and deemed "shrill" if they're too high-pitched. In the workplace, women face yet another challenge. We are less likely to ask for what we want—afraid of being labeled as bossy or emotional. Even within female-dominated spaces, misogyny can rear its ugly head, with women quick to judge each other based on outdated stereotypes.

A Historical Example of Stepping Away From Niceness: Florence Nightingale

From an early age, women are often taught to put the comfort and happiness of others before their own. It's deeply rooted in traditional gender roles, where women were expected to be caregivers, nurturers, and always accommodating.

Take the inspiring story of Florence Nightingale, born in 1820. She faced immense societal pressure to conform to the expectations of her time. Like many women of her era, her father expected her to marry young, settle down, and dedicate herself solely to the care of her husband and children. But Florence had a different calling (Alexander, n.d.).

Despite her father's objections, Florence yearned to pursue a career in nursing: a profession considered lowly and unsuitable for a woman of her social standing. She knew in her heart that caring for the sick and wounded was her true purpose. So, she boldly begged her father for just three months of schooling in nursing (Alexander, n.d.).

When Nightingale was done with her program in Germany, she trained in Paris with the Sisters of Mercy. At age 33, her name was quickly becoming recognized. In 1853, she returned to England and was made Superintendent of a hospital for "gentlewomen" in London (Alexander, n.d.).

When the Crimean War erupted in 1854, Florence saw an opportunity to make a difference. The British military hospitals were overwhelmed, lacking supplies, and plagued by unsanitary conditions. Recognizing the urgent need for skilled medical care, the secretary of war turned to Florence for help. Undeterred by the male-dominated medical establishment's reluctance to accept female nurses, Florence led a team of 38 courageous women to the frontlines. They transformed the military hospital with their compassion, expertise, and unwavering dedication to their patients' well-being (Alexander, n.d.).

Despite facing adversity and skepticism, Florence Nightingale's pioneering work revolutionized nursing and laid the foundation for modern healthcare practices. She wasn't just *nice*; she was brave, bold, and unapologetically real in pursuing her calling, even in the face of societal expectations.

Florence's story teaches us that true empowerment comes from stepping away from the constraints of niceness and embracing our inner strength. It's about setting boundaries, saying **no** when necessary, and fearlessly pursuing our passions, just as Florence did.

So, if you ever find yourself torn between social expectations and your own desires, remember Florence Nightingale's legacy. Know that you can be kind, brave, bold, and, above all, genuinely *you*. Because that's where true empowerment lies.

Societal Reinforcement

Societal reinforcement of the "nice girl" archetype is like a constant background noise that often drowns out our authentic voices. It greatly influences the perpetuation of nice girl syndrome by continually molding and validating the behaviors and attitudes that fuel it.

From a young age, we're bombarded with messages about being polite, accommodating, and pleasing to others. As we've discussed, these expectations are deeply rooted in historical and cultural perspectives, where women were expected to prioritize the needs and comfort of others above their own.

Breaking away from this societal reinforcement is no easy task. It means challenging deeply ingrained norms and beliefs, both within ourselves and within the larger community. It requires recognizing that being "nice" at the expense of our own well-being is not true kindness but, rather, a form of self-silencing and self-erasure.

In the Media

Media plays a big role in how we view the world and ourselves. Through movies, TV shows, marketing, advertising, and magazines—it shows us different types of personalities. When it comes to women, it often portrays the ideal woman as meek, self-sacrificing, and always putting others before herself. These portrayals can influence how women see themselves and how they think they should act. There is a real absence of diverse role models showcasing assertive, boundary-setting behaviors. Let's dive into how the media perpetuates the nice girl syndrome and reinforces submissive and accommodating behaviors in women:

Movies and television shows: Notice how assertive or outspoken female characters are often depicted as aggressive, "manly," or unattractive. They're sometimes portrayed as lacking warmth or likability, while the accommodating and submissive characters are seen as more endearing.

Advertising and marketing: Advertisements frequently target women with messages that reinforce traditional roles. The commercials and ads predominantly marketed toward females include cleaning products, cooking items, and childcare services—reinforcing the idea of a woman's primary sphere of influence and responsibility being within the home. Beauty and fashion ads promote ideas of perfection, linking women's self-worth to external approval and suggesting they must look a certain way to be accepted and valued.

Literature: Traditional storytelling in literature has frequently honored female figures who undergo hardship and selflessly prioritize the needs of others. These figures are commonly depicted as models of virtue, establishing a benchmark that actual women might feel compelled to follow.

Romantic comedies: These often glorify the idea of women sacrificing their own desires or boundaries for the sake of romantic relationships. The protagonist may go to great lengths to please others, often at the expense of her own well-being or originality.

Social media influencers: While social media can be empowering, it also perpetuates certain stereotypes. Influencers who conform to traditional gender roles of niceness and accommodation tend to gain more followers and popularity, reinforcing the idea that these traits are desirable.

Family Dynamics

Our families play a significant role in shaping us by instilling gendered expectations and reinforcing pleasing behaviors from a young age. Girls are often taught to prioritize politeness and compliance to maintain harmony within the family unit, receiving praise for being agreeable and avoiding conflict:

- Parents and caregivers might unknowingly reinforce pleasing behaviors by praising girls for being obedient, compliant, or accommodating.

- This constant reinforcement can embed the idea that one's worth is tied to being agreeable and avoiding conflict at all costs.

- Girls are often expected to be nurturing, empathetic, and caretaking.

- Within the family, girls may receive different messages compared to boys when it comes to expressing opinions or asserting themselves. They might be encouraged to be agreeable and avoid confrontation, while boys may be praised for being assertive and standing up for themselves.

- Within family dynamics, there may be an unspoken expectation for girls to conform to societal norms and familial expectations. This pressure to fit in and avoid standing out can lead to suppressing one's real self and conforming to others' expectations.

- Straying from these expectations may lead to exclusion or disapproval, promoting kindness over assertiveness as a more socially acceptable approach. In many societies, aggressive or confident actions by women are often viewed unfavorably, which in turn deters women from voicing disagreement or focusing on their own desires.

Education Systems

Traditional educational systems reinforcing the nice girl syndrome involve peering into how these systems often place more value on traits like compliance and obedience in girls, which can lead to the suppression of assertive behaviors and personal expression. This dynamic can contribute to the perpetuation of gender stereotypes and hinder the development of confident, autonomous individuals. Here's how:

Hierarchical structure: Educational institutions often operate within a hierarchical framework where authority figures, such as teachers and administrators, hold significant power. We are expected to follow instructions without questioning them, mirroring societal norms that discourage assertiveness, especially among girls.

Praise for obedience: In many classrooms, those who obediently follow instructions and rules are rewarded with praise, good grades, or other forms of recognition. This creates a culture where compliance is valued over independent thinking or assertiveness.

Fear of consequences: Students who dare to question rules or challenge authority may face negative consequences, such as detention, disciplinary action, or even ostracization from peers. This fear of repercussions can deter girls, in particular, from asserting themselves and speaking up for what they believe in.

Reinforcement of gender norms: Traditional schooling often perpetuates gender norms by reinforcing stereotypes about how girls should behave. Girls are encouraged to be polite, nurturing, and accommodating—while assertive behavior may be discouraged or penalized. Research indicates that teachers often treat boys and girls differently in the classroom. They tend to give more praise to boys for correct answers, while being more critical of girls for mistakes. This bias can lead to girls' knowledge being overlooked and their abilities underestimated. Additionally, teachers are more likely to commend girls for good behavior, even if it's unrelated to the lesson being taught (Erden & Wolfgang, 2004).

Workplace Environments

In workplace environments, breaking free from gendered expectations is a crucial step toward authenticity and success. Women are often socialized to take on roles that support others, such as note-taking or organizing, rather than leading. This can reinforce the idea that their primary value lies in assisting others or being accommodating. This also limits the professional growth of women and the overall effectiveness of the organization by not fully leveraging the talents of the employees:

Recognize the pressure: Understand that society often imposes gendered expectations in the workplace, pushing women toward a "nice girl" stereotype. Recognize the subtle (and not so subtle) pressure to conform to these expectations, which can limit your potential.

Awareness of gendered expectations: In the workplace, people expect men and women to behave in certain ways because of their gender. This affects how they're seen and treated. Sometimes, the same behavior is judged differently based on whether it's done by you or a man. This can lead to unfairness, where you might struggle to be taken seriously or get ahead in your careers.

Perception of assertiveness: Notice that people in the workplace see assertive behavior differently in women. When men are assertive, they're usually seen as strong leaders. But when you are assertive, you might be called aggressive or bossy.

Peer Influence

Let's explore peer influence, a terrain often underestimated yet profoundly impactful on your path to empowerment. Here, we confront the subtle yet potent forces that shape our decisions, beliefs, and aspirations—often without our conscious awareness. How does the approval or disapproval of our peers sway our choices? How does the desire for acceptance mold our sense of self? Social circles often reinforce the need we feel to be nice through subtle pressures and expectations. For example, a woman often feels the need to maintain peace and harmony within her social circle, even if it comes at her own expense. So, let's uncover the implications of peer influence more closely:

Fear of judgment: We've all felt it. That nagging worry that if we step out of line, we'll face judgment from our friends or peers. But here's the thing: Your uniqueness is your strength. Don't let the fear of judgment hold you back from being your genuine self.

Conformity vs. individuality: It's natural to want to fit in, but not at the cost of losing yourself. If your friends prioritize conformity over individuality, it's time to reassess those dynamics. Surround yourself with people who celebrate your uniqueness and encourage you to shine.

Stand out, don't blend in: Remember, you were born to stand out, not to blend in. Embrace what makes you different because that's what makes you extraordinary. The world needs your unique voice and perspective.

Romantic Relationships

In romantic relationships, it's common for women to feel pressure to conform to traditional gender roles and expectations. This phenomenon is deeply ingrained and has the potential to greatly influence personal identity, relationship dynamics, and overall well-being:

Pressure to conform: This pressure is feeling the weight of societal expectations to fulfill certain roles based on gender stereotypes. It can feel suffocating trying to fit into these molds, especially when they don't align with who you truly are. Struggling with the pressure to prioritize your partner's needs and preferences over your own leads to a loss of your own identity and desires in the relationship.

Fear of conflict: You avoid confrontation at all costs to maintain peace and harmony in the relationship, even if it means suppressing your own needs and emotions. You worry about causing discomfort or displeasure to your partner by expressing your true feelings or asserting your boundaries.

Balancing independence and connection: Struggling to find the balance between maintaining your independence and fostering intimacy and connection with your partner, it can be challenging to prioritize your own goals and aspirations while also nurturing the relationship. You feel guilty or selfish for wanting to pursue your own passions and interests, especially if they conflict with your partner's expectations or desires.

Downplaying achievements: It can be disheartening to dim your light in order to avoid rocking the boat in the relationship, tiptoeing around your accomplishments or successes to avoid emasculating your partner or making them feel inferior.

Communication breakdowns: You struggle to communicate openly and honestly with your partner about your needs, boundaries, and desires. It can feel daunting to express yourself authentically, especially if you fear judgment or rejection. Feeling unheard or invalidated, when your partner dismisses or minimizes your feelings and experiences, leads to resentment and distance in the relationship.

Psychological Underpinnings

Ask yourself how you can handle what we have discussed so far. I mean who doesn't want to embrace the fierce, real, beautiful version of themself, right? But first, let's understand the psychological underpinnings that have kept us tethered to this notion of niceness.

Need for approval and validation: Seeking validation from others becomes a default mode of operation. We crave approval like oxygen, often at the expense of our true selves.

Empowerment tip: Recognize that your worth isn't tied to others' opinions. True validation comes from within.

Conflict avoidance: The dread of conflict or disapproval can paralyze us, trapping us in a cycle of silence. We'd rather maintain the status quo than risk making waves.

Empowerment tip: Embrace the discomfort of confrontation. Your voice matters, and your boundaries deserve respect.

Low self-esteem: Our self-worth becomes intrinsically linked to how "nice" we are perceived to be. If people like us, we feel better about ourselves.

Empowerment tip: Shift your focus inward. Recognize your inherent value, regardless of others' perceptions. You are worthy simply because you exist.

Conditioning and reinforcement: From a young age, societal expectations and conditioning, especially in the age of social media, reinforce the idea that being agreeable equates to being likable and worthy.

Empowerment tip: Challenge societal norms and redefine your own standards. Your authenticity is your greatest strength.

Guilt and responsibility: We may feel guilty for asserting ourselves or setting boundaries because we perceive it as shirking our responsibility to prioritize the needs and happiness of others. This sense of responsibility is deeply ingrained through socialization, equating femininity with nurturing and self-sacrifice. As a result, women may experience guilt when they prioritize their own well-being, fearing judgment or conflict if they deviate from the role of caretaker and peacemaker.

Empowerment tip: Recognize that taking responsibility for your own well-being and happiness is not selfish but essential for personal growth and fulfillment. Practice setting boundaries and asserting your needs with compassion and confidence, understanding that advocating for yourself is a fundamental aspect of self-care.

These psychological underpinnings can be complex, but they don't define us. They're merely parts of our story toward empowerment. It's time to put the constraints of "niceness" behind us and step boldly into our authenticity.

The Traits of Nice Girl Syndrome

Do you recognize the subtle but powerful force pushing you to prioritize others' needs over our own, to fear saying *no*, and to constantly seek validation through perfectionism? Nice girl syndrome might be a part of who you are. There are some common traits associated with it.

People-Pleasing

Do you ever find yourself agreeing to things you don't really want to do? It can be tough to say *no* sometimes. Maybe your friend asks you to go out, but you're really tired and just want to stay home. Instead of being honest, you say *yes* to avoid disappointing them. Saying *yes* all the time might make you feel overwhelmed. It's okay to say *no* sometimes. Your friends will understand if you need rest.

Do you ever put aside what you want to do in order to please someone else? Maybe your sibling wants to watch a movie you don't like, but you agree to watch it with them anyway. It's great to make others happy, but it's also important to think about what you want. Don't forget to take care of yourself too. It's okay to compromise and find activities that make both you and your loved ones happy.

Do you ever feel bad when you decide to do something for yourself instead of helping someone else? It's common to feel guilty, but self-care is essential. Taking care of your own needs doesn't mean you don't care about others. It's like when you're on a plane that experiences trouble; when emergency oxygen masks come down, you need to secure your oxygen mask before helping others. Prioritizing yourself allows you to be more present and supportive to the people around you.

Perfectionism

Perfectionism is when you set really high standards for yourself. You might expect things to be perfect all the time, which can make you feel stressed. It's like when you're writing and you erase a sentence over and over because it's not exactly right. You might worry that others will judge your work, so you keep fixing it. Perfectionism can sometimes hold you back from finishing tasks, as you keep trying to perfect them.

When you are a perfectionist, you might want everything to be flawless. You might think that anything less than perfect is a failure. For example, if you're drawing a picture, you might keep erasing and redoing parts that aren't exactly how you want them. This can make your work take a lot longer than needed, and you might even feel frustrated because it's not turning out as perfect as you imagine in your mind.

Another aspect of perfectionism is being really hard on yourself when you make mistakes. If you're writing a story and you make a spelling mistake, you might feel like you're not good enough as a writer. Perfectionism can lead you to always feel like you're inadequate. You might compare your work to others and feel like they are better than you.

Fear of Failure

Women, in particular, may fear rejection due to societal expectations that place a high value on being likable, agreeable, and accommodating. This fear stems from the belief that asserting oneself or setting boundaries may lead to disapproval, criticism, or even abandonment by others.

In the context of the nice girl syndrome, the fear of rejection often drives individuals to prioritize the comfort and happiness of others over their own needs and desires. They may avoid expressing their true thoughts or feelings, fearing that doing so will result in rejection or conflict. This can lead to a pattern of people-pleasing behavior, where individuals suppress their own authenticity in order to gain acceptance and approval from others.

The fear of rejection perpetuates the cycle of the nice girl syndrome by reinforcing the belief that one's worth is dependent on the approval and validation of others.

Putting Others First

Neglecting yourself to care for others is a common tendency people have. You may find yourself prioritizing the needs of others above your own. It's like always putting others in the front seat of the car, letting them decide where to go and how fast to drive. This can leave you feeling exhausted and drained, like a phone battery at 1% after a long day of heavy usage.

It's easy to lose sight of your own needs when you're busy catering to the needs of others. Picture yourself in a busy train station, always making sure others catch their trains while you keep missing yours. This self-neglect can lead to burnout and a feeling of emptiness inside.

Sometimes, you might equate your value with how much you can do for others— for example, an over-responsibility for others. You might find yourself taking on more than a fair share of responsibility in relationships or tasks to ensure everything goes smoothly or to prevent others from having to go through discomfort or inconvenience. It's like measuring your self-worth with a ruler that only counts the good deeds you do for others. When you choose to ignore your own needs to prevent conflict or confrontation with others, you're pushing your well-being to the side. It's like being a referee in a game who always lets others break the rules just to keep the peace, even if it means sacrificing your own fairness and integrity.

Body Image Issues

Body image issues pertain to our perceptions of our physical appearance and the thoughts and feelings that come with it. It's common to compare ourselves to the often unrealistic standards of beauty portrayed in the media and on social platforms.

When you constantly measure yourself against flawless images of models or celebrities on magazines or social media, you might feel like you don't measure up. Comparisons like these often lead to feelings of low self-esteem and inadequacy. Remember, many of these images are heavily edited or airbrushed to fit an ideal that is often unattainable in real life.

Feeling ashamed or embarrassed about how you look can be a heavy emotional burden. It's crucial to understand that beauty comes in various shapes, sizes, and forms. Embracing your uniqueness and individuality can help you appreciate your appearance for what it is, rather than what you believe it should be based on societal expectations.

Negative thoughts about your body can impact your overall well-being. They can limit your participation in enjoyable activities, prevent you from socializing, and hinder your confidence. Instead, focus on self-acceptance and self-care. Engage in activities that make you feel good about yourself, and surround yourself with positive influences that lift you up.

Hypervigilance

Experiencing hypervigilance can make a person constantly worry about how others see them. It's like being hyper-aware of what people are thinking about you, all the time. This might mean you spend lots of time worrying about the impressions you make and how others react to you.

One aspect of hypervigilance is seeking approval from those around you. This means you are always looking for confirmation or validation from others. For example, you might frequently ask others for their opinions on your actions or seek reassurance that you are doing things right. This behavior can stem from a deep need for acceptance and the overwhelming desire to be liked, which drives much of the behavior aimed at pleasing others. This can lead to constantly seeking external validation.

People experiencing hypervigilance tend to overanalyze their social interactions. This could involve replaying conversations in your mind or dissecting every word and gesture during a social encounter. For instance, you might wonder if you said something wrong or if others perceived you in a negative light, even when there is no concrete evidence to support these worries.

Difficulties Setting Boundaries

Setting boundaries can be tough. Boundaries help define how much you are willing to give and receive in relationships. Sometimes, you feel obliged to say *yes* even when you really want to say *no*. Maybe a friend asks a favor, but you're already overwhelmed. Saying *yes* in such situations can lead to stress and exhaustion. It's important to learn to say *no* without feeling guilty. Remember, it's okay to prioritize your well-being.

Asserting your own needs can bring up feelings of guilt or selfishness. You might worry that, by setting boundaries, you're letting others down. However, it's crucial to prioritize self-care. Consider this: If you don't take care of yourself, how can you be there for others? By valuing your needs, you set a positive example for those around you.

Another difficulty in setting boundaries is allowing others to overstep them without speaking up. Perhaps a colleague consistently interrupts your work, but you stay silent to avoid conflict. It's essential to communicate your boundaries clearly. By expressing your limits, you show respect for yourself and enable others to understand your needs.

◆ Exercise ◆

Journal Exercise: Unveiling Your Nice Girl Patterns

Using a journal, delve into the layers of nice girl syndrome, uncovering its roots and manifestations in your life. By raising awareness, you pave the way for transformation and liberation from the confines of niceness.

Find a quiet space, and allow yourself to dive deep into your thoughts and memories. Be honest, be brave, and remember that this is your safe space for self-exploration.

Childhood Chronicles

Reflect on your upbringing and the messages ingrained in you during your formative years. Consider the following prompts:

- What were the expectations placed upon you by your parents or guardians?

- Recall any specific incidents or recurring themes from your childhood related to niceness.

Unmasking Media Influence

Explore the impact of media on your perception of niceness and femininity. Analyze the messages you've internalized from various media sources:

- What types of media do you frequently consume (e.g., movies, TV shows, magazines, social media)?

- How do these sources depict idealized versions of women and their behaviors?

- Reflect on instances where you've felt pressured to conform to societal norms perpetuated by the media.

Confronting Approval-Seeking Behaviors

Confront the psychological factors driving your approval-seeking behaviors. Dive into your fears, insecurities, and tendencies to seek validation:

- Identify two recent situations where you've prioritized others' approval over your own needs and desires.

- What underlying fears or insecurities might be fueling these approval-seeking behaviors?

- Reflect on how these behaviors manifest in your relationships and interactions with others.

Congratulations on completing this journey of self-reflection. By uncovering how nice girl syndrome impacts your life, you've taken the movement toward reclaiming your authenticity and agency. Remember, you are worthy of setting boundaries, saying *no*, and embracing your true self. Stay courageous; stay empowered.

It is time to turn the page and get ready to explore constant pleasing and how much it is costing you. How is it truly impacting your life?

2

The Cost of Constant Pleasing

People-pleasing is a trait many of us have grown accustomed to, often without realizing its true toll on our lives. As women, we've been taught that being kind, agreeable, and flexible is the best way to earn approval and affection. But is it worth it?

I want you to picture yourself at a gathering, and someone asks if you can stay a little later to help clean up. Despite being exhausted and having a two-hour drive home, you agree with a smile. Or perhaps it's a colleague asking for your help on a project, and even though your plate is already overflowing, you say *yes*—fearing the consequences of refusal more than the burden of added work.

These are just glimpses into the everyday scenarios where people-pleasing rears its head. This often becomes second nature for most. After all, saying *yes* seems easier than dealing with potential conflict or disappointing others. But herein lies the trap: The more we prioritize others' happiness over our own, the more we lose sight of our own needs, desires, and boundaries.

In this chapter, we're going to unravel the cost of constant pleasing. We'll explore the insidious ways in which this behavior chips away at our well-being, leaving us feeling drained, resentful, and disconnected from our authentic selves. Let's set the scene with a story.

Michelle is always eager to help. From office tasks to social gatherings, she never says *no*. Her schedule is full of commitments for others, leaving her with very little time for herself. While many see Michelle as kind and generous, the truth is that she is overwhelmed and finding it hard to cope with the pressure she puts on herself.

Each morning, Michelle wakes up early to tackle her long to-do list. She rushes through her day, ensuring that everyone around her is taken care of. At work, she volunteers for multiple committees, taking on extra projects without hesitation. Her colleagues praise her for her dedication, but Michelle's own well-being takes a backseat in the process.

Michelle's constant need to please others has become a heavy burden. She finds herself saying *yes* to tasks that she doesn't have time for, simply because she can't bear to disappoint anyone. The pressure to maintain her reputation as a reliable and accommodating person weighs heavily on her shoulders, causing stress and anxiety to build up over time.

Despite her outward appearance of competence, Michelle struggles silently with her overloaded schedule. She battles exhaustion and burnout, trying to keep up with the demands she has imposed on herself. The lack of time for self-care and relaxation takes a toll on her mental and physical health, leading to a cycle of fatigue and emotional strain.

Michelle's pattern of people-pleasing and nice girl syndrome is a common one for many who prioritize others' needs over their own.

Did you see any similarities in Michelle's story? Many do. Why don't we spend some time looking at how people-pleasing can impact your life and explore how it manifests in daily life. We will follow this up by learning valuable lessons that will empower you to break free from constant pleasing and reclaim your sense of self-worth and power.

Understanding People-Pleasing Behavior

At its core, people-pleasing is all about seeking approval and validation from others by bending over backward to meet their expectations, even if it means sacrificing your own happiness and well-being in the process. It's like being stuck in this never-ending loop of trying to keep everyone else happy.

People-pleasing is a behavioral tendency characterized by a strong desire to please others, frequently disregarding one's own wants, limits, and needs. People-pleasers typically go to great lengths to avoid conflict, rejection, or disapproval—seeking validation and acceptance through accommodating others' wishes and preferences. This pattern of behavior often involves saying *yes* to requests or demands even when it's not in your best interest, prioritizing others' happiness over your own well-being. People-pleasing can become ingrained as a habitual response to social situations, leading to feelings of resentment, exhaustion, and a loss of authenticity over time (Huntington, n.d.).

Is Our Brain Wired for People-Pleasing?

In understanding why our brains are wired for approval, it's crucial to dive into the fascinating world of neuroscience. Our brains, magnificent and intricate as they are, have evolved over millennia with one primary goal: survival. And guess what? Survival isn't just about finding food and shelter. It's about forming connections with others.

From the moment we're born, our brains are wired to seek approval and validation. Why? Because, at its core, connection equals safety and belonging. Think of it this way: Back in the day, our ancestors roamed the earth in tribes. Being part of a tribe meant you had protection, access to resources, and a better chance of survival. Those who were isolated or ostracized from their tribes faced significant challenges.

Dr. Matthew Lieberman, a leading neuroscientist, shed light on this phenomenon. His research at UCLA revealed that social connection is not just a luxury—it's a necessity. In fact, lacking meaningful connections can be as harmful to our health as smoking! Our brains are wired to crave social interaction as much as they do food and water (Suttie, 2013).

So, how does this wiring work? Mirror neurons are neurons that allow us to instinctively mimic the actions and emotions of those around us. Ever noticed how yawning seems contagious? That's your mirror neurons in action, forging a subtle bond between you and even strangers in your vicinity (Carey, 2018).

Just as our brains revel in social connection, they recoil from social pain. Rejection, criticism, or a sense of disconnection can trigger the same areas of the brain associated with physical pain. Let's discuss dopamine, the brain's favorite feel-good chemical. When we receive external validation—a compliment or a nod of approval—our brains light up like fireworks. Dopamine floods our system, bathing us in warmth and reassurance. It's addictive, really (Jen, 2023).

Our brains are creatures of habit, constantly seeking out patterns and routines. So, when seeking approval becomes a habit, our brains latch onto it like a well-worn path through the forest. We crave that dopamine hit, perpetuating a cycle of seeking approval to feel validated.

Let's rewind a bit and explore the impact of relationships on our quest for validation. From a young age, many of us are taught that deviating from societal expectations invites trouble. Whether it's disapproval from peers, criticism from family, or the dreaded shame spiral, the message is clear: Be nice or face being rejected or disapproved.

Over time, this external pressure erodes our trust in ourselves. Self-doubt becomes our constant companion, whispering in our ears whenever we dare to stray from the norm. And so, we seek approval to quell that nagging doubt and to reassure ourselves that we're not alone in our choices.

Breaking free from the cycle of seeking validation is not about denying our innate need for connection. It's about striking a balance and recognizing that, while validation from others is nice, true validation comes from within. It's about nourishing self-awareness, embracing our uniqueness, and standing tall in our authenticity.

It is important to understand that our brains are wired to seek approval and avoid conflict. Psychologically, it's firmly embedded in a complex interaction of emotional needs, early life experiences, and learned behavior patterns. Psychological origins frequently originate from deep-seated fears, desires for acceptance, and the need for security. Understanding this concept helps us realize that people-pleasing is not merely a personal trait but a multifaceted response shaped by profound psychological factors, innate inclinations, and societal expectations. This broader perspective enables us to explore more effective strategies for managing and transforming these patterns.

Social Conditioning

Social conditioning starts at a young age when we begin to hear messages about being "nice" and "polite." It's like a rulebook handed to us by society, dictating that we should always prioritize others. Saying *no* is often seen as a faux pas, almost like it is morally wrong! This societal norm ingrains in us the habit of putting everyone else's needs above our own, even if it's detrimental to us. The pressure to please others is pervasive in our lives.

We observe these behaviors in our families and tend to learn repetitive behavior that avoids conflict in favor of those for approval, communities, culture, and media—further reinforcing the belief that prioritizing others is the right thing to do. The fear of being judged or rejected pushes us to conform to societal standards of niceness and selflessness.

Constantly prioritizing others over ourselves can have a detrimental impact on our mental and emotional well-being. It is essential to strike a balance between being kind and considerate to others while also taking care of our own needs. Establishing boundaries and mastering the art of saying *no* when needed are essential for preserving a strong sense of self.

Self-Worth

A healthy sense of self is rooted in internal self-assurance, where one's self-esteem is nurtured by a deep understanding and acceptance of oneself. It's about having confidence in your own worth, independent of external validation or approval from others. When self-esteem relies on external validation, it becomes fragile, leading to people-pleasing behaviors as a means to sustain a sense of value and identity. When we feel like we're not good enough, we often look for approval from other people. It's kind of like constantly trying to show that we are important—one small favor, or one people-pleasing moment, at a time. The way we were loved and supported when we were young can affect how we think about ourselves and how we compare ourselves to everyone else. If we didn't get enough praise when we were growing up, we might feel unsure about ourselves and look for it from others to show that we are valuable. Learning where these feelings come from can help us build a stronger sense of accepting ourselves and lessen the need for approval from other people.

If we received a lot of love and encouragement, it's likely that we feel more secure in who we are. However, if we didn't get much support, we might struggle with feeling confident and find ourselves looking to fill that by pleasing others. For example, if a person wasn't praised for their achievements growing up, they might feel like they constantly need to prove themselves to feel worthy.

When we start to recognize that our past experiences have shaped our need for approval, we can start focusing on building self-acceptance. This can involve developing a stronger sense of self-worth by recognizing our own strengths and values, rather than relying on others to affirm them.

Attachment Theory

The way we learned to relate to people during our formative years plays a significant role in how we handle conflicts later in life. If we were accustomed to receiving positive reinforcement and support as children, we are more likely to not need the constant validation from our peers as adults. We have a strong sense of self. If a problem arises, we feel confident in knowing we can deal with it. On the other hand, if our early relationships were marked by conflict and turmoil, we may develop strategies like people-pleasing to avoid confrontation in our adult interactions.

We don't often give too much thought to how our relationships in childhood can have such a lasting influence on how we interact with others in adulthood. The experiences we have while growing up shape the way our brains are wired, impacting our need for approval and our approach to conflict resolution.

So, it's no wonder we find ourselves stuck in the people-pleasing trap. Awareness is a vital step to breaking free. Once we understand the psychological roots of our people-pleasing tendencies, we can start challenging those ingrained beliefs and behaviors. We can learn to set boundaries, prioritize our own needs, and cultivate authentic connections based on mutual respect and understanding.

Emotional Impact of People-Pleasing

Liz was raised by her grandmother: a prim and proper lady who believed in old-fashioned values and the power of being "nice" above all else.

From a young age, Liz was taught that a girl's place was in the home, not the workplace. Men belonged in the office, while women belonged in the kitchen, making sure everything was perfect and everyone was happy. Liz was groomed to be pretty, polite, and accommodating, and to always put others' needs before her own.

Growing up, Liz never dared to raise her voice or express her opinions too loudly. She learned to keep her head down, smile through discomfort, and never make a fuss. After all, *nice girls are meant to please everyone they meet.*

As Liz grew older, she found herself drawn to a career as a secretary, where her skills of organization and efficiency were valued. She became the epitome of the perfect secretary—always reliable, always helpful, and always smiling. But behind that smile lurked a sense of emptiness and a feeling that she was living life on autopilot, going through the motions without truly feeling alive.

In her personal life, Liz fell into a toxic marriage with a man who mirrored the expectations set by her grandmother. He expected her to be the perfect wife—silent, submissive, and always ready to cater to his needs. But as the years passed, Liz realized that her own needs were never being met. She longed for love, respect, and understanding, but her husband seemed incapable of providing any of those things.

The emotional toll weighed heavily on Liz. She felt trapped, suffocated by the expectations placed upon her by society, by her grandmother, and by her husband. The word *no* has no place in her world. If asked to host holiday dinners, she had to say *yes*. If asked to work late, only cook her husband's favorite meals, maintain the entire home, or run errands for her friends and family—she had to say *yes*. This is how she felt important. This is how she felt loved.

One day, in a moment of clarity, Liz made a bold decision. She sought out support, turning to a life coach who helped her rediscover her sense of self-worth and inner strength.

With their guidance, Liz learned to set boundaries, to say *no* without guilt, and to prioritize her own happiness above the expectations of others.

As Liz continued to learn the importance of self-discovery, she realized that being nice was not the same as being kind. True kindness came from a place of authenticity—from honoring oneself and others with honesty, compassion, and respect.

With each step she took towards reclaiming her power, Liz felt a sense of liberation wash over her. She learned to love her flaws, her imperfections, and her quirks—knowing that they were what made her beautifully human.

Today, Liz is living her life boldly and authentically, being unapologetically herself in every way. She is no longer bound by the confines of niceness but, instead, she radiates a warmth and kindness that comes from deep within her soul.

And as Liz looks back, she knows that breaking up with niceness was the best decision she ever made. For in letting go of the need to please others, she found the freedom to truly be herself.

Do you ever feel like you have to put constant effort into just making sure everyone around you is happy? That's the reality for many people-pleasers, and it is emotionally draining.

First, there's the anxiety that comes with it. You're always worrying about whether you're doing enough, saying the right thing, or being there for everyone all the time. It's like living with a constant knot in your stomach, never really feeling at ease because you're so focused on making sure everyone else is.

Then, there's the insecurity. When you're always seeking approval from others, it's easy to start doubting yourself. You start questioning whether you're good enough as you are, without constantly catering to everyone else's needs. It's like your self-worth becomes tied to what others think of you, which is a pretty shaky foundation to build your confidence on.

When you're constantly second-guessing yourself to make sure you're meeting everyone else's expectations, it's hard to trust your own instincts. Welcome, self-doubt. You start to wonder if you're making the right decisions or if you're just pleasing others at your own expense.

All of these feelings are like weights dragging you down, holding you back from truly being yourself. You deserve to live a life that's authentic to you, not one that's dictated by the opinions of others. In the next chapter, we will dissect exactly how to break free from people-pleasing behavior.

Mental Health Consequences

When we're constantly aiming to please others, it's like living life on a treadmill that never stops. The pressure to always say *yes*, to always be accommodating and to be "nice," can take a serious toll on our mental health.

Let's break it down:

Stress: I want you to picture that your to-do list is a mile long, and on top of that, you've said *yes* to helping out with three different projects, even though you're already stretched thin. Can you relate? Trying to be that people-pleaser leads to overwhelming stress. Your mind is in a constant state of "What if I let them down?" Stress hormones flood your system, wreaking havoc on your mood, energy levels, and overall well-being. Let's look more on how this impacts our physical health below.

Depression: The constant need for approval and fear of disappointing others can spiral into feelings of inadequacy and worthlessness. When your self-worth is tied to others' validation, it's a slippery slope to feeling like you're never good enough. This can manifest as symptoms of depression—such as persistent sadness, loss of interest in activities, and feelings of hopelessness.

Burnout: Imagine a candle burning at both ends; that's burnout, in a nutshell. You're giving all your time and energy to everyone else, leaving nothing for yourself. Eventually, the flame fizzles out, and you're left feeling exhausted, emotionally drained, and disengaged from life. Burnout not only affects your mental health but also your physical health, leading to symptoms like insomnia, headaches, and even weakened immune function. We will explore more on that below.

Chronic people-pleasing can lead to a serious case of identity confusion. We get so caught up in being what others want us to be that we lose sight of who we truly are. It's like wearing a mask all the time and, eventually, we forget what's underneath.

And then, there's the perfectionism trap. People-pleasers often feel like they need to be perfect in order to gain approval and validation from others. We set these ridiculously high standards for ourselves, and when we inevitably fall short (because, let's face it, nobody's perfect), we beat ourselves up over it. It's a never-ending cycle of striving for the unattainable, and it can really mess with our mental health.

Studies show that people-pleasing can negatively affect women's abilities to thrive. We know that all genders of people-pleasers can fall into unhealthy, toxic, or even abusive relationship patterns—cultural expectations that women always be pleasant and oriented toward others, and not themselves—causing mental health issues (Gattuso, 2018).

By recognizing the connection between people-pleasing and these mental health consequences, we can start to break free from the cycle. Remember, it's okay to prioritize yourself, sometimes; in fact, it's essential for your mental health and overall happiness.

Physical Impact on Health and Well-Being

When you're constantly trying to please everyone else, your body goes into overdrive. Your cortisol levels skyrocket, your heart rate goes up, and your muscles tense up like a coiled spring. Over time, this chronic stress can wreak havoc on your body, causing psychosomatic symptoms. You could experience things like:

Heart issues: Prolonged stress can elevate your chances of developing heart disease and stroke. It elevates your blood pressure and cholesterol levels, putting extra strain on your heart.

Weakened immune system: When you're stressed, your immune system takes a hit, making you more susceptible to infections, viruses, and even chronic illnesses.

Digestive issues: Ever notice how stress can make your stomach churn? That's because stress messes with your digestive system, leading to issues like stomachaches, indigestion, and irritable bowel syndrome (IBS).

Fatigue: Constantly putting others' needs ahead of your own can leave you feeling drained and depleted. You might find yourself feeling exhausted, even after a full night's sleep, because you're not giving yourself the chance to recharge and rejuvenate.

Skin problems: Stress can trigger or worsen skin conditions like acne, eczema, or psoriasis. Your skin might act up when you're under pressure, serving as a visible reminder that your body is feeling the effects of emotional stress.

Weight gain or loss: Stress can throw your appetite out of balance, leading to either overeating or undereating. Plus, it can cause your body to store fat, particularly around your midsection.

Muscle tension and pain: Ever heard of stress knots? They're those little spots of tension that can crop up in your neck, shoulders, and back when you're feeling stressed. Over time, this muscle tension can lead to chronic pain and stiffness.

Headaches: Tension headaches or migraines can be exacerbated by stress and suppressed emotions. You might find yourself experiencing frequent headaches when you're overwhelmed or feeling pressured to please others.

Sleep problems: Stress and sleep don't exactly go hand in hand. It can make it harder to fall asleep, stay asleep, or get restful sleep—leaving you feeling tired and groggy during the day.

Accelerated aging: Chronic stress can actually speed up the aging process, both internally and externally. It can lead to wrinkles, gray hair, and even shorten your telomeres—the protective caps on your chromosomes that help keep your cells healthy and youthful (Yegorov et al., 2020).

The thing is, when you're so focused on making everyone else happy, you forget about the most important person in the equation: yourself. It's like trying to fill up everyone else's cup while yours is running on empty.

One major way people-pleasing can affect you physically is through exhaustion. I'm talking bone-deep, soul-crushing exhaustion. You're so busy saying *yes* to everyone else that you forget to listen to your own body's cries for rest and rejuvenation.

Then, there's the issue of neglecting self-care. When you're constantly focused on making others happy, your own needs tend to fall by the wayside. You might skip meals, neglect exercise, or forget to take time for activities that bring you joy.

And let's not forget about those unhealthy coping mechanisms. When you're constantly putting on a happy face for others, it's easy to turn to things like food, alcohol, or even drugs to numb the underlying feelings of stress and overwhelm. But these quick fixes only serve to mask the problem temporarily, while exacerbating it in the long run.

Studies indicate that individuals with people-pleasing traits frequently encounter elevated levels of chronic stress and anxiety. The continuous effort to fulfill the expectations of others and the pursuit of external approval may result in a persistent state of stress. Prolonged periods of stress can trigger an overactive immune response, causing it to target not just external dangers but also healthy cells and tissues (Dhabhar, 2014).

Breaking Free From People-Pleasing Patterns

We have uncovered a lot of information about the connection between nice girl syndrome and people-pleasing behaviors. You may have noticed yourself in some of the scenarios.

In the upcoming chapters, we're going to examine the heart of nice girl syndrome and explore how to reclaim your power by setting boundaries and saying *no* with confidence. We'll tackle the fear of disappointing others, the guilt that comes with asserting your needs, and the importance of prioritizing self-care without apology.

Through relatable anecdotes, practical tips, and empowering exercises, you'll learn to recognize the signs of people-pleasing behavior, understand its roots, and, most importantly, discover strategies to break free from its grip. You'll uncover the beauty of authenticity, the strength in setting healthy boundaries, and the joy that comes from honoring your own needs and desires.

◆ Exercise ◆

Journal Exercise: Unleashing Your Authentic Self

Using your journal, let's explore an exercise designed to identify and explore people-pleasing behaviors and embrace your bold, authentic self.

Step 1: Reflect on Past Instances

Think back to those moments when you felt like you were constantly on a hamster wheel of pleasing others. What were the circumstances surrounding these instances?

Were you saying *yes* when you really wanted to say *no?*

How did it feel in your gut?

Any knots or butterflies?

And, perhaps most importantly, did you walk away from those situations with a heavy heart or a sense of regret?

Step 2: Identify Triggers and Patterns

Now, let's dig a little deeper. Are there certain people or situations that always seem to trigger your people-pleasing tendencies? Maybe it's your overbearing boss, your well-meaning but boundary-crossing friend, or even your own inner critic.

What underlying fears or beliefs are driving this urge to please?

Are you afraid of rejection, conflict, or not being liked? And do you notice any recurring patterns in your interactions? Patterns are like breadcrumbs leading us to the root of the issue.

Step 3: Challenge Your Beliefs

What do you believe about yourself and your worth?

Are you worthy of love, respect, and fulfillment just as you are?

How about relationships? Are they meant to drain you or lift you up?

And finally, are there any sneaky beliefs or expectations that you've picked up along the way that no longer serve you? It's okay to let go of what no longer resonates with your true self.

Remember, this exercise isn't about beating yourself up for past behaviors. It's about shedding light on those old patterns so you can break free and step into your power. So, grab that journal, pour your heart out, and get ready to rewrite your story on your own terms. You've got this, warrior!

3

Redefining Self-Care

For far too long, societal norms have perpetuated the notion that niceness equates to perpetual self-sacrifice—a formula destined for burnout, resentment, and profound depletion. It's time we rewrite this narrative and reclaim our entitlement to self-care.

First, let's dispel a prevalent myth: Self-care is not synonymous with selfishness. Let's engrave this mantra into our consciousness: Self-care is not selfish. Rather, it forms the bedrock of a richly fulfilling and purposeful existence. It entails recognizing your intrinsic value, validating your own needs, and extending to yourself the same grace and compassion generously bestowed upon others.

In the pages ahead, we'll deconstruct the true essence of self-care and elucidate its indispensable role in fostering mental, emotional, and physical well-being. We'll equip you with practical insights and actionable strategies to seamlessly integrate self-care into the tapestry of your daily life, irrespective of the demands crowding your schedule.

What Is Self-Care?

Self-care is about consciously taking care of our physical, emotional, and mental well-being. It's about recognizing our own needs and taking proactive steps to meet them. It is essential for our overall health and happiness.

But why do so many of us struggle with self-care? Well, there are a few reasons.

The Definition You Have Is Likely False

For years, self-care was synonymous with "care of self," meaning simple acts like taking your medication or regular exercise. However, today's culture inundates us with a new definition: indulging in prolonged pleasurable activities aimed at achieving peace, happiness, and beauty, often showcased through social media hashtags.

In theory, this modern interpretation sounds delightful, filled with activities we enjoy. Yet, it demands substantial energy and adherence to a specific process with a specified outcome: creating a tranquil space, immersing in mindfulness and reflection, and emerging refreshed with a glow of self-love.

Despite the roots of self-care emphasizing practices to preserve health and well-being, the pressure to achieve self-improvement through trendy self-care can feel overwhelming and utterly exhausting. This expectation leads to a paradox. We tell ourselves to embrace #selfcare but find ourselves too drained to engage in it.

You Believe Putting Yourself First Means Putting Everyone Else Last

From an early age, we learn about opposites. We are taught the difference between happy and sad, awake and asleep. This binary thinking often persists into adulthood, leading us to believe that prioritizing ourselves means neglecting others.

New relationships—whether with a new partner, a baby, a boss, or even a friend—often triggers a tug-of-war between our time and responsibilities, compelling us to sacrifice our own needs. Those early lessons teach us that we need to be "nice" and please these people in our lives, but how can we possibly take care of them *and* ourselves?

You Think It's Too Expensive

In today's consumer-driven culture, the message echoes: the more expensive, the better. As self-care gains popularity, so does the belief that it requires lavish expenditures. Think fancy organic candles and soft, cooling sheets—exclusive products to soothe and relax you.

This narrative perpetuates the misconception that self-care is a privilege reserved for the affluent, leaving many feeling excluded. However, genuine self-care transcends materialism; it encompasses practices that enhance well-being, many of which are accessible and cost-free.

While an indulgent spa day may be a form of self-care, so too is a brief yoga session from a free online tutorial. Self-care isn't about luxury; it's about intentionally engaging in activities that nurture our physical and mental health.

Self-care doesn't necessitate extravagant spending. It involves deliberate actions tailored to our well-being, regardless of financial constraints.

You Don't Know When to Do It

Society extols the virtues of hard work, promoting a "push-through-it" mentality. This ethos permeates various aspects of life, discouraging vulnerability and prioritizing resilience.

However, this mindset, coupled with nice girl syndrome, often leads to suppressing emotions, hindering our ability to recognize our own needs.

Without self-awareness, implementing self-care becomes daunting. How can we care for ourselves if we're unaware of what requires attention?

Embracing self-care involves reshaping our relationship with emotions, viewing them not as weaknesses but as valuable insights. With practice, emotions cease to be obstacles; they become guides, directing us toward areas of our lives that warrant care and attention.

There May Be Barriers in the Way

You may have noticed that, in certain cultures or societies, there's a stigma attached to putting your own needs first. This societal pressure often steers people away from prioritizing self-care, nudging them instead to constantly meet the expectations of others—be it family, work, or community.

You need to continue to challenge these societal norms and welcome the concept of self-care. This will help create a more fulfilling and rewarding life.

Who Has the Time?

Managing the complexities of modern life—including busy schedules, demanding professional obligations, and familial responsibilities—often presents barriers to the practice of self-care. In this dynamic landscape, you can frequently find yourself grappling with the challenge of prioritizing personal well-being and the incessant demands of external pressures.

Because of the responsibilities, it becomes all too common for people to defer their own needs in favor of fulfilling obligations to work, family, and other facets of life. However, it's imperative to recognize that neglecting self-care can have detrimental effects on both physical and mental health, ultimately hindering overall growth and fulfillment.

In the pursuit of genuine self-care, it is essential to approach the allocation of time and resources with a strategic mindset. By proactively carving out dedicated moments for rejuvenation and reflection, you can foster resilience and growth in the face of life's challenges.

Your Access May Be Limited

Access to self-care practices can face significant hurdles due to a multitude of factors. Financial constraints often present a substantial barrier, as certain self-care activities may come with associated costs that are prohibitive for some with limited resources. Additionally, a lack of knowledge about what self-care resources are available can impede one's ability to engage in practices. This may stem from inadequate education or awareness regarding the importance of self-care and the variety of accessible options.

Those living in environments where opportunities for self-care are scarce may face additional challenges. Such environments may lack essential infrastructure or community support systems that facilitate the pursuit of self-care. Limited access to green spaces, recreational facilities, or mental health services can exacerbate feelings of isolation and diminish the likelihood of engaging in self-nurturing activities.

Types of Self-Care

When we pinpoint the specific aspect of our life that requires additional attention, we can effectively establish a self-care routine or practice to cater to it. For instance, if you realize you are experiencing some loneliness, taking a quiet bath with some scented candles may not necessarily provide comfort. In this case, self-care could involve reaching out to an old friend by phone, even if you're calling from the bathtub.

There was a study done in 2021 where researchers were quoted as saying that "self-care in a healthcare setting means the ability to care for yourself through:

- awareness

- self-control

- self-reliance" (Hullett, 2023, para. 6).

Taking care of yourself is obviously crucial for leading a well-balanced, healthy, and joyful life. While research on self-care is limited at present, the above existing knowledge is quite encouraging.

There are five types of self-care and each type is interconnected, forming a robust foundation for your holistic well-being. As you prioritize self-care in every aspect of your life, you'll discover newfound confidence, resilience, and fulfillment in your journey toward living boldly and authentically. Let's explore the five types of self-care, each pivotal in nurturing your overall well-being and empowerment:

Physical self-care: Taking care of your body is the cornerstone of holistic wellness. This involves regular exercise, nourishing your body with proper nutrition, ensuring adequate sleep, maintaining good hygiene practices, and scheduling regular medical checkups. Physical well-being isn't just about fitness; it's about boosting mood, reducing stress, and enhancing cognitive function. When you prioritize physical self-care, you're investing in your vitality and resilience. Some activities could include (Hullett, 2023):

A. getting a massage

B. keeping yourself hydrated

C. creating a comfortable sleep space

D. permission to take naps

E. a healthy cooking class

Emotional self-care: Nurturing your emotional health is essential for maintaining balance and resilience in the face of life's challenges. This involves rituals such as practicing self-compassion, expressing your emotions authentically, setting boundaries to protect your emotional space, engaging in activities that bring you joy, and seeking encouragement from your support network when needed. When you prioritize emotional self-care, you foster greater self-awareness, develop healthier coping mechanisms, and build deeper connections with yourself and others. Maybe give the following emotional self-care activities a try to get you started (Hullett, 2023):

F. showing gratitude

G. having a good cry

H. journaling your feelings

I. doing things that bring you joy

J. learning a new skill or hobby

K. talking about your feelings with those you trust

Social self-care: Human connection is a fundamental aspect of well-being. Social self-care involves nurturing meaningful relationships and fostering connections with others. This includes spending quality time with loved ones, engaging in social activities, volunteering, and seeking out supportive communities. Building a strong support network not only reduces feelings of loneliness but also enhances emotional resilience and overall satisfaction in your interpersonal relationships. Some ways to kick-start this are (Hullett, 2023):

L. joining a team or group

M. scheduling a game night with friends

N. asking someone you trust when you need help

O. cuddle time with your fur baby

P. volunteering

Q. planning dates with partners, friends, and family

Spiritual self-care: Spiritual well-being goes beyond religious practices; it's about what feeds your soul and brings you a sense of fulfillment and purpose. This could involve connecting with a higher power, engaging in creative expression, practicing gratitude, communing with nature, or participating in community service. Prioritizing spiritual self-care provides a sense of grounding and perspective—fostering resilience and inner peace amidst life's challenges. To practice this, why not try (Hullett, 2023):

R. a quiet walk in nature

S. practicing affirmations

T. journaling

U. meditating

Mental self-care: Caring for your mental well-being is crucial for maintaining cognitive function, managing stress, and fostering resilience. This includes practices such as mindfulness meditation, journaling, pursuing creative hobbies, continuous learning, and challenging negative thought patterns. By prioritizing mental self-care, you enhance your problem-solving abilities, cultivate emotional stability, and improve your overall quality of life. Your mental health is a gateway to your overall health, so why not try (Hullett, 2023):

V. reading a great book

W. doing a social media withdrawal

X. listening to a podcast

Y. trying a new hobby

Z. taking an art class

When you embrace all five types of self-care, you empower yourself to break free from the constraints of "nice girl syndrome" and embrace a life of authenticity, boldness, and genuine self-care.

Practical Self-Care Strategies

It is imperative to equip ourselves with practical self-care strategies. These strategies, far from being a one-size-fits-all solution, are tailored to individual preferences, lifestyles, and requirements—serving as a personalized toolkit ready to manage life's diverse challenges.

By relinquishing the outdated notion that niceness necessitates self-abnegation, you reclaim agency and independence in your interactions and relationships. You learn to assert boundaries without apology, and to articulate needs without guilt.

Let's explore some empowering ways to prioritize yourself:

Establish a Self-Care Routine

Spending time every day on activities that make you feel good is important for taking care of yourself. This could be doing a short meditation when you wake up in the morning, writing in a journal before bed, or relaxing with a book. These simple actions help you look after your mental and physical well-being, as well as your inner self. Begin by:

Starting your day right: In the morning, before the busyness of the day takes over, consider giving yourself a moment to breathe and clear your mind. A morning meditation can be as short as 5–10 minutes. Find a quiet spot where you won't be disturbed, sit comfortably, and focus on your breath. Let go of any worries or thoughts that are swirling in your mind, just for this brief period. This can help set a positive tone for your day ahead.

Unwinding in the evening: After a long day, it's beneficial to wind down and relax before going to sleep. Journaling in the evening can be a great way to reflect on your day, jot down your thoughts and feelings, or simply empty your mind onto paper. This can be particularly helpful if you tend to overthink things. Writing down your thoughts can create a sense of clarity and calm, preparing you for a restful night's sleep.

Be consistent: Making self-care activities a part of your daily routine is crucial. Consistency helps you establish a habit, allowing these moments to become an integral part of your day. Prioritizing self-care every day means you are investing in your well-being, which can have a positive impact on your overall quality of life.

Prioritizing Sleep

Get ready to transform your life by making sleep your number one focus. It's time to treat sleep like the valuable asset it is. Begin by crafting a relaxing bedtime routine that tells your body it's time to wind down. Maybe that involves reading a few pages of a calming book, sipping on a cup of herbal tea, or doing some gentle stretching. Find what relaxes you and make it a nightly tradition. Start by:

Optimizing your sleep environment: Set the stage for a restful night's sleep. Your sleep environment plays a vital role in the quality of sleep you get. Invest in a cozy mattress that supports your body and makes you feel like you're sleeping on a cloud. Ensure that your room is a peaceful sanctuary by keeping it dimly lit or dark, if possible. Block out any noise that might disrupt your slumber, whether it's by using earplugs or a white noise machine.

Consistent sleep schedule: Again, being consistent when it comes to getting the most out of your sleep is what will make this a habit. The trick is finding what works for your regular sleep schedule and sticking to it—going to bed and waking up at the same time each day. This aids in regulating your body's internal clock, which helps you easily fall asleep and wake up feeling refreshed.

Mindful Living

Mindfulness is about being present in each moment, fully aware of what's happening inside and around you. This involves intentionally paying attention, with no judgment. These activities can help you stay grounded, reduce stress, and improve your overall well-being. Why not try the following to get started:

Meditation: Meditation is a common practice to nurture mindfulness. You can start by finding a quiet place to sit or lie down comfortably. Close your eyes, concentrate on your breath, experience the feeling of each inhalation and exhalation, and gently guide your mind back to your breath if it strays. Taking just a few minutes each day to meditate can help reduce stress and increase mental clarity.

Deep breathing exercises: This is an effective way to enhance mindfulness. Find a comfortable position, close your eyes, and take a deep breath in through your nose, letting your belly rise. Hold the breath for a few seconds, then exhale slowly through your mouth. Repeat this process several times. Deep breathing can help calm your mind and body, promoting relaxation and reducing anxiety.

Getting into nature: Spending time in nature is a powerful way to practice mindfulness. Take a walk in a park, sit by a river, or simply spend time outdoors. Notice the sounds of birds chirping, the smell of fresh air, and the beauty of the natural world around you. Connecting with nature can help you feel more grounded and present in the moment.

Journaling for self-reflection: Keeping a journal can be a helpful tool for practicing mindfulness. Jot down your feelings, thoughts, and experiences without judgment. Use your journal to reflect on your day, set intentions, or express gratitude. Regular journaling can enhance self-awareness, promote emotional processing, and support personal growth.

Mindful eating: Mindful eating is a practice that encourages you to bring full attention to your meals. Begin by acknowledging the smells, textures, and flavors of your food. Take small bites and chew slowly, savoring each mouthful. By being mindful while eating, you can enhance your digestion, appreciate the nourishment your food provides, and even notice when you're full—preventing overeating. This practice can transform mealtime into a moment of mindfulness and gratitude.

Benefits of mindfulness: Engaging in mindfulness practices can have numerous benefits for your mental and emotional health. When you cultivate present moment awareness, you may find that your stress levels decrease as you learn to let go of worries about the past and future. Mindfulness can also enhance your focus and concentration, allowing you to engage more fully in tasks and activities. Furthermore, by deepening your connection with yourself and others, you can foster stronger relationships and a greater sense of empathy.

Incorporating mindfulness into daily life: To make mindfulness a part of your daily routine, start with small steps. Set aside a few minutes each day for meditation or deep breathing exercises. Practice mindful eating by savoring at least one meal without distractions. As you become more comfortable with these practices, you can gradually incorporate mindfulness into other aspects of your life, such as walking, driving, or interacting with loved ones. The key is to approach each moment with intention and open awareness.

Stay Hydrated and Eat Nutritious Foods

Drinking water is super important for your body to work well. It helps with things like digestion, skin health, and concentration. If you don't drink enough water, you might feel tired or get headaches. Other good options for hydrating fluids are things like herbal teas or coconut water. It is imperative to incorporate the following, as well:

Nutrient-rich foods: Eating foods that have lots of good nutrients in them is key for feeling your best. Think colorful fruits like berries or oranges, tasty vegetables like spinach or carrots, and foods like brown rice or quinoa that give you energy. Including lean proteins like chicken or beans can help your muscles stay strong.

Balanced diet: It's really important to eat a mix of different foods to stay healthy. Try to have a little bit of everything, including a variation of vegetables, fruits, grains, and proteins. Eating a range of foods helps make sure you get all the vitamins and minerals your body needs to keep you going strong.

Supporting your health: By choosing foods that give your body the goodness it needs, you're looking after yourself in the best way possible. Good food can make a big difference in how you feel each day, making you more energized and focused. Avoid skipping meals and remember: You deserve great health and wellness.

Engage in Regular Physical Activity

Engaging in regular physical activity is vital for your overall well-being. Finding joy in movement is key to making exercise a sustainable part of your routine. You can choose enjoyable forms of exercise that make you feel good. This could be a simple activity like taking your dog for a walk in a park or yourself around your neighborhood. The fresh air and change of scenery can help clear your mind and lift your spirits. Another option is to try a rejuvenating yoga session. Yoga is a gentle way to improve flexibility, strength, and mindfulness. You could also put on your favorite music and have a dance party in your living room. Dancing is a fun and effective way to get your heart rate up and release stress. Here are some other important things to keep in mind:

Boost mood and energy levels: Regular physical activity benefits not only your body but also your mind. When you move your body regularly, it releases endorphins, referred to as the hormones that can have you feeling better in no time. These endorphins can boost your mood, reduce feelings of anxiety and depression, and increase feelings of happiness. Additionally, staying active can increase your energy levels. You may find that after a workout or a physical activity session, you feel more alert, focused, and ready to take on the day.

Overall well-being: Prioritizing regular physical activity contributes to your overall well-being. When you make exercise a part of your daily routine, you are investing in your long-term health. Physical activity can help maintain a healthy weight, strengthen your muscles and bones, and improve your cardiovascular health. By engaging in various forms of movement regularly, you are promoting a healthy lifestyle that supports your physical and mental health.

Setting Boundaries

Understand the importance of setting boundaries. When you're trying to move away from the nice girl syndrome, it's vital to recognize your own needs and ensure that they are met. Setting boundaries involves clearly defining what is acceptable and what isn't in your interactions with others. It's about safeguarding your time, energy, and emotional well-being. Keep the following at the forefront of your mind:

Honoring your needs: Learn to prioritize yourself by setting boundaries that honor your needs. This means being assertive and saying *no* when necessary. If you're constantly saying *yes* to things that don't align with your values or goals, you will burn out. By respecting your limits and boundaries, you empower yourself to focus on what truly matters to you.

Saying *no* gracefully: It's essential to learn how to decline commitments in a gracious and respectful manner. Saying *no* doesn't indicate selfishness; it just signifies you prioritize your time and energy. Practice saying *no* politely but firmly. For example, you can express gratitude for the opportunity while remaining firm as to why you can't commit. Remember, setting boundaries is about respecting yourself and your needs.

Overcoming guilt: Breaking away from the nice girl syndrome involves overcoming feelings of guilt when you prioritize yourself. Understand that it's okay to put yourself first and that self-care is what will keep you healthy. Remind yourself that you deserve to set boundaries that protect your well-being and that saying *no* is an act of self-respect.

Seek Support

Seeking support is essential when facing difficult times. Don't be afraid to ask for help from those around you, whether it's your friends, family members, or mental health professionals. Sharing your feelings and reaching out for guidance can help you become stronger and more connected with others. It's okay to lean on your support system when you need a listening ear or a comforting presence. Here are some great tips to keep in mind:

Reach out to friends and family: During tough situations, your friends and family can be your pillars of support. They can offer a shoulder to lean on, provide valuable advice, or simply be there to listen to your concerns. By expressing your thoughts and emotions to them, you can lighten the burden you're carrying and gain new perspectives on how to tackle challenges.

Connect with mental health professionals: Sometimes, the support of mental health professionals can be extremely beneficial. These trained experts can offer specialized guidance, therapy, or counseling to help you manage your emotions and thoughts effectively. Don't hesitate to seek therapy or mental health support if you feel overwhelmed or if you need professional assistance in coping with difficult situations.

Benefits of seeking support: Opening up to others and seeking assistance can have numerous benefits. It can promote resilience and the ability to bounce back from adversity by providing you with coping strategies and emotional support. Additionally, sharing your struggles with a trusted individual can create a sense of connection and strengthen your relationships.

Engage in Hobbies and Leisure Activities

When you find yourself constantly pleasing others and neglecting your own needs, it's important to remember to enjoy life and pursue activities that make *you* happy. This can involve various hobbies and leisure activities that allow you to relax and unwind. Consider the following:

Prioritize activities that spark joy: Discovering activities that ignite your passions can bring a sense of fulfillment and contentment to your life. By prioritizing hobbies that bring you joy, you can create moments of happiness and relaxation amid your busy schedule. For example, painting, writing, or playing a musical instrument can serve as creative outlets that help you express yourself and unwind after a long day.

Cultivate a garden for relaxation: Tending to a garden can be a therapeutic and rewarding hobby that allows you to connect with nature. When you are mindful to plant, it not only makes your surroundings more beautiful but also offers a sense of accomplishment as you witness the growth and progress of your plants. Spending time in the garden can be a peaceful and calming experience, offering a chance to recharge and de-stress.

Immerse yourself in creative pursuits: Engaging in creative pursuits—such as crafting, sculpting, or DIY projects—can unleash your artistic side and boost your creativity. These activities allow you to explore new ideas, experiment with different materials, and unleash your imagination. Creating something with your hands can be a satisfying and rewarding experience, allowing you to tap into your artistic talents and skills.

Practice Self-Compassion

Self-compassion means being kind and understanding toward yourself, particularly when you face tough times or doubt yourself. It involves treating yourself with the same care and empathy you would offer to those you encounter in your life. This approach helps you build resilience and acceptance of yourself:

How to embrace self-compassion: One way to practice self-compassion is to acknowledge your feelings without judgment. For instance, if you're feeling sad or anxious—instead of criticizing yourself for feeling that way—accept your emotions with kindness. You can tell yourself it's normal to feel this way and offer words of comfort, as you would to a friend in distress.

Being understanding: In moments of adversity, avoid being too hard on yourself. Show understanding by reminding yourself that everyone makes mistakes or feels overwhelmed at times. Treat yourself with patience and compassion, knowing that you're doing the best you can in the given circumstances.

Nurturing a supportive inner dialogue: Developing a supportive inner dialogue is key to practicing self-compassion. Pay attention to how you speak to yourself internally. Replace self-criticism with words of encouragement and understanding. By cultivating a positive and gentle inner voice, you create a nurturing environment for self-growth and self-acceptance.

Take Breaks and Rest

Consider the signals your body sends you, and respect when you feel tired or in need of some time to unwind. It's important to break away from your tasks, periodically, and give yourself space to relax and recuperate. You can start by including short breaks in your daily schedule to avoid burnout and maintain your energy levels. These breaks could be as simple as stepping away from your desk every hour, taking a short walk outside, or engaging in a quick stretching routine to release tension from your muscles. Consider the following:

Understanding your body's needs: Being attuned to your body's signals is crucial for maintaining overall well-being. When you start feeling fatigued or mentally drained, it's a sign that your body requires rest. Consider this as an opportunity to pause, reflect, and allow yourself time to recharge. By acknowledging and responding to these signals promptly, you can prevent reaching a point of exhaustion that may hinder your productivity and health in the long run.

Incorporating restful practices: Incorporating moments of rest and relaxation into your routine is key to sustaining a healthy work–life balance. Find activities that help you unwind and rejuvenate, whether it's engaging in mindfulness exercises, meditation, or spending quality time with loved ones. By consciously making time for activities that bring you joy and peace, you create space for mental clarity and emotional well-being.

Finding balance through rest: Balancing work commitments with restful practices is a continuous process that requires mindful attention. Reflect on your daily routines and identify areas where you can insert moments of rest without feeling guilty or anxious about downtime. Remember that productivity is not solely measured by constant activity but also by your ability to recharge and approach tasks with renewed energy and focus.

When you choose to integrate these empowering self-care strategies into your life, you will see the differences self-discovery, resilience, and authentic living can make in your life. Embrace the power of prioritizing yourself and watch as your life blossoms with vitality, purpose, and fulfillment.

◆ Exercise ◆

Journal Exercise: Self-Care Inventory

This empowering exercise is designed to establish and grow a life filled with genuine self-care. We're about to create your personal roadmap to bold authenticity.

Step 1: Create a Self-Care Wheel

Use a blank page in your journal and draw a large circle, dividing it into sections like slices of a pie. Label each section with one of the five types of self-care: physical, emotional, mental, social, and spiritual. This wheel will serve as the blueprint for your self-care journey.

Step 2: Reflect on Each Area

Take a moment to sit with each aspect of self-care and explore what it means to you. Ask yourself and answer the following questions.

What activities or behaviors support my physical well-being?

What do I do presently to nurture my emotional health?

What do I practice to help me maintain mental focus and clarity? Reflect deeply on each slice of the pie.

Step 3: Identify Self-Care Practices

Now, let's brainstorm. Within each section of the self-care wheel, jot down specific self-care practices or activities that resonate with you. Whether it's a brisk walk in the morning sun, journaling your thoughts and feelings, meditating to clear your mind, scheduling coffee dates with cherished friends, or connecting with nature—let your imagination run wild.

Step 4: Set Goals and Action Steps

You've identified your self-care practices; now, it's time to turn them into actionable steps. Choose one or two practices from each category that you're eager to prioritize. Put specific goals and actionable steps for incorporating these practices into your daily or weekly routine. Remember, small steps lead to significant transformations. For example, each Wednesday I will meditate for 15 minutes. Once a week I will meet with friends for coffee. For twenty minutes each day, I will do something that brings me joy.

Step 5: Reflect and Adjust

Regularly revisit your self-care inventory to assess your progress. Celebrate any and all changes you have implemented that lean into your self-care and be gentle with yourself in times of setback. If necessary, adjust your goals and action steps to align with your evolving needs and desires.

Congratulations for taking this bold step toward genuine self-care. Embrace this journey with courage and compassion, knowing that you're reclaiming your power and honoring your authentic self.

59

4

The Art of Saying *No*

This is a pivotal chapter dedicated to mastering the art of assertive communication. If you're reading this, chances are you've experienced the internal tug-of-war between your desire to please others and your need to honor your own boundaries. It's a familiar struggle for many women, who often feel the weight of societal expectations to be nice and accommodating at all costs.

Within these pages we will look at redefining our relationship with the word "no." Contrary to popular belief, saying *no* is a fundamental aspect of self-care and self-respect. When you master the skill of assertive communication, you find the power to prioritize your well-being without succumbing to guilt or resentment. It assists others in comprehending your boundaries and valuing your time, space, and resources.

Meet Heidi, a woman who wears her "Nice Girl" badge proudly. From her early days, she learned that saying *yes* was the surest way to gain approval and love. Growing up, Heidi was always eager to help her family with chores, never wanting to disappoint her parents. In school, she volunteered for every project, eager to be seen as helpful and cooperative by her teachers and peers. This pattern followed her into adulthood, where Heidi found herself saying *yes* to every request that came her way.

At work, Heidi was the go-to person for her colleagues. Need someone to cover a shift? Heidi would do it. Have an extra project that needs completing? Heidi would take it on without hesitation. Her coworkers admired her dedication, but what they didn't see was the toll it was taking on her. Heidi would stay late at the office, sacrificing her own personal time to help others.

In her personal life, Heidi's friends relied on her for emotional support. They knew that Heidi would drop everything to be there for them in times of need. Whether it was listening to their relationship woes or helping them move, Heidi was always there with a willing heart and open arms.

Even in her romantic relationships, Heidi struggled to assert herself. She found herself staying in relationships long past their expiration date, afraid to hurt her partner's feelings by saying *no* to their needs and desires. She would sacrifice her own happiness and well-being in the name of keeping the peace and avoiding conflict.

Physically and emotionally exhausted, Heidi found herself at a breaking point. She realized that her inability to say *no* was not only affecting her own health and happiness but, also, preventing her from living authentically and boldly. It was time for a change.

Heidi made the decision to lean on the guidance of a life coach and began investing in self-discovery and empowerment, learning the importance of saying *no*. She discovered that true self-care meant honoring her own needs and desires, even if it meant disappointing others, at times. With the support of friends, family, and her coach— Heidi started to reclaim her time, energy, and sense of self-worth.

She no longer felt burdened by the expectations of others and, instead, she embraced the opportunity to live life on her own terms. By breaking up with niceness, Heidi discovered the true power of self-care and boldly stepped into a life that is authentic, fulfilling, and uniquely her own.

Embracing *No* on a Personal Level

Understanding the significance of saying *no* goes beyond recognizing its utility in managing our external commitments; it's also about acknowledging its profound impact on our personal well-being. Saying *no* isn't just about declining an invitation or refusing a request—it's about setting boundaries, preserving our energy, and safeguarding our mental and emotional health. It frequently serves as a stepping stone to personal development.

Every time you say *yes* to something you don't want to do, you're saying *no* to yourself. You're saying *no* to your own needs, desires, and priorities. You're prioritizing external expectations over your inner voice, compromising your authenticity in the process.

The personal ramifications of this can be significant. When we consistently say *yes* to others at the expense of ourselves, we erode our self-worth and diminish our sense of agency. We become disconnected from our true selves, navigating life on autopilot rather than actively engaging with our own desires and passions.

Furthermore, the emotional toll of people-pleasing and overcommitment can't be ignored. Resentment simmers beneath the surface as we begrudgingly fulfill obligations that empty us of our vitality. Anxiety creeps in as we juggle an overwhelming array of tasks and responsibilities, fearing the consequences of disappointing others.

Physically, the toll of perpetual *yeses* can manifest in stress-related symptoms such as fatigue, and headaches. Our bodies bear the burden of our inability to say *no*, signaling to us the urgent need to reassess our priorities and reclaim our power.

On a deeper level, the inability to say *no* perpetuates a cycle of self-neglect and disempowerment. We lose sight of our own needs and aspirations, allowing the expectations of others to dictate the course of our lives. Our relationships suffer as a result, lacking the authenticity and reciprocity that comes from genuine self-expression and mutual respect.

In essence, the personal impact of saying *no* extends far beyond the immediate context of any given situation. It touches every aspect of our lives—shaping our sense of self, our relationships, and our overall well-being. Recognizing this impact is the first step toward reclaiming our agency and embracing a life guided by authenticity and self-care.

The Importance of the Word *No* in the Workplace

Navigating the terrain of saying *no* in the workplace can feel like a tightrope walk, especially when you're early in your career or deeply passionate about your work. The weight of guilt often hangs heavy, leaving you questioning your role as a team player or fearing disappointment from your manager. This sense of guilt can morph into fear. If you say *no*, you may then be overlooked for promotions or viewed as never wanting to help the team.

However, mastering the art of saying *no* is a vital skill for professional success. It's not just about protecting yourself from being overburdened or taken advantage of; it's also about safeguarding the passion and drive that fuels your career. Far too often, enthusiastic employees fall into the trap of saying *yes* to everything, only to find themselves drained, disillusioned, and resentful of the job they once found fulfilling. Have you ever found yourself saying *yes* to everything, only to then come up short? Are you then perceived as a failure? Piling too much on your plate because you can't say *no* puts you in direct fire of not being able to meet expectations. You risk damaging your credibility and the trust placed on you by your colleagues and supervisors.

Moreover, there are instances where saying *no* becomes a crucial act of self-preservation. Whether it's facing unrealistic demands or being asked to engage in tasks that compromise your integrity, saying *no* establishes firm boundaries and reaffirms your commitment to ethical conduct. Yet, it's essential to approach this with clarity and confidence.

Before declining a task, it's imperative to grasp your actual responsibilities. Take time to review your job description, discuss priorities with your manager, and seek clarification if necessary. Ensure that your reluctance isn't stemming from a fear of the unknown but, rather, from a genuine understanding of your capacity and obligations.

Crafting your refusal requires finesse. Here's how:

"I would love to help, but I don't have the capacity at the moment."

This response not only acknowledges the request but also sets a clear boundary. By honestly addressing your workload and priorities, you avoid overcommitting yourself while leaving the door open for future collaboration.

Additionally, establishing boundaries before taking leave is crucial. Communicate clearly with your team and clients, ensuring they understand your availability and responsibilities during your absence.

"I will be on leave then, so I won't be able to do that."

This direct response emphasizes the importance of respecting personal time off, preventing misunderstandings or last-minute demands.

If you find yourself burdened with an excessive workload, reflect on whether the task aligns with your career goals or exceeds the boundaries of your role. Establishing transparent expectations with your team and manager is key to preventing recurring issues.

"I appreciate the offer; however, I'm unable to commit to that right now."

Expressing gratitude while declining a task maintains professionalism while setting boundaries and preserving your capacity for future opportunities.

In situations where ethical concerns arise, don't hesitate to seek guidance from company policies or trusted colleagues. If discomfort persists, speak up and propose alternatives that align with your values.

"I'm not comfortable doing that; is there anything else I can assist with?"

This response communicates discomfort while offering solutions aligned with your values and comfort level, ensuring your well-being remains a priority.

In embracing the power of *no*, you reclaim autonomy over your time, energy, and professional trajectory. When you set boundaries rooted in self-respect and integrity, you pave the way for a career defined by fulfillment, purpose, and authenticity.

The ramifications of overcommitment can be profound, affecting various facets of our lives. When we habitually accept every demand, our resources become stretched thin. We find ourselves juggling myriad obligations, experiencing overwhelm and a dearth of equilibrium.

Yet, there exists an alternative path—one that entails establishing firm boundaries and exercising the ability to decline when necessary. By embracing this approach, we reclaim agency over our time, energy, and self-worth.

Consider the dividends of setting boundaries and articulating negative responses with confidence. Through the delineation of clear limits, we carve out space to concentrate on our priorities. This deliberate focus allows for a deeper engagement with our own aspirations and fosters a heightened sense of contentment and fulfillment.

By declining excessive commitments, we unlock a precious commodity: time. This abundance affords opportunities for meaningful interactions with loved ones, the pursuit of personal interests, and dedicated self-care. Liberated from the compulsion to constantly appease others, we find comfort in the realization that prioritizing ourselves is not only permissible but essential.

Crucially, by establishing boundaries and exercising the right to decline, we affirm our own worth and agency. Through this affirmative action, we grant ourselves the latitude to live life on our own terms, unapologetically.

Heidi's journey serves as a compelling testament to the transformative potential of saying *no*. By fostering the ability to set boundaries and honor her own needs, she transcended the confines of societal expectations, forging a path that resonated authentically with her true self.

Overcoming Guilt and the Sense of Obligation

To break free from the constraints of nice girl syndrome, one of the most formidable obstacles we face is the weight of guilt and the sense of obligation. These emotions can act as massive barriers, preventing us from asserting our needs and setting boundaries that are essential for our well-being. Uncovering the psychological roots of guilt and obligation can help equip us with strategies to overcome them.

The Psychological Landscape

Women are taught to prioritize the needs and desires of others over their own. This ingrained sense of obligation often leads to a fear of disappointing or rejecting others, driving us to prioritize external validation over our own internal well-being. Breaking free from this cycle requires a deep understanding of the psychological factors at play and a willingness to challenge societal norms that dictate our behavior. These include:

Prioritizing self-care: Central to overcoming guilt and obligation is the recognition and prioritization of our own needs. This isn't an act of selfishness but, rather, a fundamental aspect of self-care. By acknowledging and tending to our own well-being, we empower ourselves to show up more fully in our relationships and pursuits. It's important to cultivate a mindset that values self-compassion and recognizes that setting boundaries is an act of self-respect, not selfishness.

Challenging negative beliefs: Guilt often stems from negative beliefs and thought patterns that tell us we're not doing enough or that our needs aren't valid. It's crucial to challenge these beliefs and reframe our perspectives. By practicing self-compassion and acknowledging our worthiness, we can gradually shift our internal narrative and cultivate a mindset of empowerment.

Strategies for liberation: Breaking free from the grip of guilt and obligation requires intentional action. This might involve setting boundaries with compassion and assertiveness, surrounding ourselves with supportive individuals who respect our individuality, and engaging in practices that nurture our emotional well-being. By taking small, deliberate steps toward prioritizing our own needs and desires, we can begin to untangle ourselves from the chains of societal expectations and embrace a life of authenticity and fulfillment.

The next chapter is dedicated to uncovering practical aspects of boundary-setting. But for now, remember that your needs are valid, your worthiness is inherent, and you deserve to live a life that honors your authenticity and self-worth.

Building Resilience and Confidence

Have you ever marveled at someone's ability to gracefully navigate through life's ups and downs? Perhaps you've wondered what gives them that unwavering confidence and resilience in the face of challenges. Well, let me assure you, it's not some elusive trait reserved for the chosen few. Resilience and confidence are skills that can be honed and nurtured, much like a muscle that grows stronger with exercise.

Resilience is often described as the ability to bounce back from setbacks, to weather the storms of life with grace and fortitude. But it's not just about bouncing back; it's also about bouncing forward, emerging from adversity stronger and more resilient than before. It's about facing challenges head-on, knowing that you have the inner resources to overcome them.

Picture a sturdy tree swaying in the wind. Despite the force of the storm, it remains rooted firmly in the ground, bending but never breaking. That's resilience in action. Like the tree, we too can learn to bend without breaking and adapt to life's ever-changing circumstances with resilience and grace.

The Role of Confidence

Confidence stands as the linchpin of assertive communication and boundary-setting. Consider a scenario where you find yourself needing to assert a boundary or speak up for yourself in a room full of individuals. The manner in which you conduct yourself, the tone of your voice, and the conviction behind your words all derive from your confidence.

Confidence is not synonymous with loudness or dominating conversations; rather, it epitomizes a profound belief in one's intrinsic worth and value. When one is confident, the ability to set boundaries and assert oneself becomes a natural expression of self-respect. It entails recognizing that one's needs and feelings are valid and deserving of consideration.

The significance of confidence in this context can be delineated as follows:

Self-worth: Confidence is intrinsically tied to one's self-worth, which is the deep-seated recognition of one's own value and worthiness. This level of self-recognition is not merely about feeling good about yourself; it's an acknowledgment that you have inherent value that does not diminish based on external circumstances or opinions. This recognition enables a person to approach interactions with a robust sense of entitlement to respect and consideration. Confident people feel empowered to voice their opinions, ask for what they need, and decline requests without guilt or hesitation. They assert their views and negotiate for themselves—not out of arrogance, but from a stable understanding that their needs are as important as others'. This fundamental belief is crucial because it helps in maintaining a balanced and healthy interpersonal dynamic, where communication is direct and respectful.

Clarity: Confident individuals have a clear understanding of their values, priorities, and boundaries. This clarity enables them to communicate effectively and assertively, as they remain steadfast in their convictions and intentions.

Authenticity: Authenticity is the hallmark of assertive communication. Confidence enables us to express ourselves genuinely, free from the constraints of external judgment or societal expectations.

Resilience: Confidence acts as a shield against the fear of rejection or disapproval. It provides the inner strength needed to navigate any pushback or negative reactions that may arise from setting boundaries or expressing needs, allowing individuals to stay true to themselves despite external pressures.

To build confidence and enhance assertive communication and boundary-setting skills, consider the following strategies:

Self-awareness: Start by engaging in introspection to gain a deeper understanding of yourself. Reflect on your values, strengths, and boundaries. Ask yourself what matters most to you, what you excel at, and where you draw the line. Self-awareness forms the bedrock upon which confidence is built. By knowing yourself more intimately, you can better navigate various situations with authenticity and conviction.

Practice assertiveness: Begin by asserting yourself in low-stakes situations. This could involve setting boundaries with friends, colleagues, or family members in scenarios where the consequences are minimal. Practice saying *no* when necessary or expressing your needs and preferences respectfully but firmly. Each assertive act, no matter how small, serves as a catalyst for the growth of confidence. With each successful interaction, you'll gain momentum and feel more empowered to assert yourself in increasingly challenging situations.

Positive self-talk: Challenge negative self-talk and replace it with empowering affirmations. Monitor your inner dialogue and pay attention to the messages you're sending yourself. Whenever you catch yourself engaging in self-doubt or criticism, consciously reframe those thoughts into positive affirmations. Remind yourself of your worth, capabilities, and past successes. Foster a mindset that reinforces your value and potential. By adopting a more positive and affirming self-talk, you'll gradually build a stronger sense of self-confidence.

Celebrate achievements: Acknowledge and celebrate every instance where you successfully set a boundary or communicated assertively. Take time to reflect on these accomplishments and recognize the courage and strength it took to assert yourself. Whether it's saying *no* to an unreasonable request, expressing your needs in a relationship, or standing up for yourself in a challenging situation—each achievement is a testament to your growing confidence. By celebrating these milestones, you not only acknowledge your progress but also reinforce your belief in your ability to assert yourself effectively in the future.

Approach this with patience and self-compassion, knowing that with confidence as your ally, you will move through life's challenges with poise, authenticity, and resilience.

Technique for Fostering Resilience and Confidence

Fostering resilience and confidence requires a multifaceted approach. When you integrate these skills into your daily life, you can acquire the inner strength and confidence needed to break free from nice girl syndrome and embrace authentic self-care. Let's take a closer look at those skills:

Celebrating successes: Acknowledging and celebrating achievements, regardless of size, is a foundational practice in building resilience and confidence. Each success serves as a testament to one's capabilities and strengths. By intentionally recognizing these accomplishments, you nourish a positive self-image and reinforce a belief in your ability to overcome challenges. Encourage the habit of celebrating both personal and professional victories, reinforcing the notion that every step forward is a significant achievement worthy of recognition.

Seeking support from others: In moments of challenge or uncertainty, seeking support from trusted individuals can provide invaluable perspective and encouragement. This network may include friends, family members, mentors, or professional coaches. By reaching out for guidance and emotional support, you gain insight into your experiences and find reassurance in knowing you are not going through this alone. Fostering meaningful connections with supportive people grows resilience by providing a safe space for vulnerability and validation.

Embracing adaptability: Developing resilience entails embracing adaptability as a core skill. Life is inherently unpredictable, and setbacks are inevitable. However, those with resilience possess the ability to pivot in the face of adversity, remaining steadfast in their pursuit of personal and professional growth. Continue to practice reframing challenges as opportunities for learning and innovation, fostering a mindset that thrives on change rather than fearing it. By cultivating adaptability, you grow more confident.

Practicing self-compassion: Central to building resilience and confidence is the practice of self-compassion. Too often, we internalize self-criticism and judgment, hindering our ability to bounce back from setbacks. Practice self-compassion by treating yourself nicely, with understanding and acceptance, especially in moments of difficulty. When you acknowledge your humanity and inherent worth, you develop a resilient inner dialogue that bolsters your confidence.

✦ Exercise ✦

Assertive Self-Care Role-Playing Exercise

Objective: To equip you with practical strategies for saying *no* assertively but respectfully, through role-playing exercises that simulate real-life scenarios.

Materials needed:

- Cue cards you can write various situations requiring assertive refusal on
- Timer to manage role-playing sessions
- Debriefing worksheet for reflection

Instructions:

Setting the stage:

- Find a comfortable and quiet space where you can focus without distractions.
- Remind yourself that the purpose of this exercise is to empower you to assertively communicate your boundaries and needs.

Practical strategies for saying *no*:

- Reflect on past experiences where you struggled to assert yourself: maybe a boss that continues to push your commitments, or a family member that unloads burdens on you without considering how it impacts you.
- Reflect on what assertive responses you could have used in those different situations, focusing on clarity, firmness, and respect. For example, "Thank you for considering me; however, I am currently at my workload capacity and need to prioritize my current commitments." Or consider, "I value our time together and appreciate your friendship.

However, it's important to me that we respect each other's time. In the future, I'd appreciate it if we could agree on a specific meeting time and both make an effort to be punctual."

Role-playing scenarios:

- Using your cue cards, create your own scenario cards based on a recent or anticipated situation.
- Role-play the scenario, taking on both the role of the requester and the assertive responder.
- Practice delivering your assertive response, paying attention to your tone, body language, and confidence.

Handling pushback:

- Anticipate potential pushback or negative reactions to your assertive response.
- Write down strategies for responding to pushback with grace and firmness, while maintaining your boundaries. For example, If the other person expresses disappointment or frustration, acknowledge their feelings while standing firm in your boundaries. For instance: "I understand that you're disappointed, and I appreciate your perspective. However, my decision stands because it's important for me to prioritize my own well-being." This strategy would be "acknowledge and validate." You could consider, restate boundaries, or offer alternatives.

Reinforcing assertive boundaries:

- Reflect on how you can reinforce assertive boundaries in your daily interactions.
- How can you communicate your boundaries consistently and confidently, both verbally and non-verbally? For example, using "I" statements, or being clear and direct.

Debrief and reflection:

- After each role-playing session, take a few moments to reflect on your experience.
- Identify areas where you felt confident and areas where you could improve your assertiveness.
- Determine what insights and lessons you learned from the exercise, and celebrate your progress toward assertive self-care.

Remember, assertiveness is a skill that takes practice and perseverance. Keep challenging yourself to assert your boundaries and prioritize your own needs. With each assertive interaction, you're one step closer to living boldly and authentically.

5

Setting Healthy Boundaries

In the place of personal development, few things are as essential and empowering as the setting of boundaries. As you go through the complexities of modern life, you may often find yourself confronted with demands and expectations, both external and internal. In the pursuit of harmony and connection, you can inadvertently sacrifice your own well-being, surrendering our autonomy and agency at the altar of niceness.

You can redefine the narrative and reclaim your power. Drawing upon my own experience and that of those around me, I have borne witness to the potential that arises when we set healthy boundaries.

In this chapter, we will explore the different aspects of boundaries, explaining their importance in building genuine relationships, maintaining mental and emotional balance, and enhancing self-esteem. Armed with the knowledge and tools provided, you will be empowered to recognize your own boundaries, identify instances of boundary violation, and handle complexities of interpersonal dynamics with clarity and confidence.

The Importance of Healthy Boundaries

Boundaries are the invisible fences that delineate our personal space, needs, and values. They are the guardians of our emotional well-being and the gatekeepers of our inner sanctuary. Yet, for many of us, the concept of boundaries may be unfamiliar territory, obscured by the fog of societal expectations and the relentless pursuit of niceness.

We now know that, as women, we are often conditioned from a young age to prioritize the needs and desires of others above our own. We are taught that being "nice" equates to being worthy of love and acceptance. However, this belief system leads us where? Down a perilous path of self-neglect and emotional martyrdom.

Up to this point we have uncovered the myriad manifestations of nice girl syndrome, from the relentless pursuit of approval to the self-sacrificial art of people-pleasing. We explored the pivotal role of self-care in nurturing our inner radiance and reclaiming our power. And we bravely confronted the daunting task of saying *no* with grace and conviction.

Now, as we move deeper into the heart of self-discovery, we confront the indispensable role of healthy boundaries in our quest for liberation and self-actualization. Learning to set healthy boundaries can help you shield yourself from the onslaught of toxic influences and ground you in your authentic truth.

When overcoming the nice girl syndrome, setting boundaries becomes paramount. It's about shifting from being a people-pleaser to becoming a self-lover.

This means prioritizing yourself. It means recognizing that setting boundaries is an act of self-love and self-respect. It's about acknowledging your own needs and honoring them without apology.

But why are healthy boundaries so crucial on this journey of self-liberation?

Self-esteem boost: Asserting boundaries is a direct affirmation of your worth and value in the world. By clearly delineating what is acceptable and unacceptable in your interactions and relationships, you send a powerful message to yourself and others that you are deserving of respect and consideration. When you consistently uphold your boundaries, you cultivate a deep sense of self-worth that serves as the foundation for healthy self-esteem. This self-esteem boost emanates from the knowledge that you are worthy of being treated with dignity and kindness, both by yourself and those around you.

Emotional well-being: Boundaries act as a protective shield against emotional overwhelm and burnout. In a world where demands and expectations can feel incessant, boundaries create essential space for you to prioritize your mental and emotional health. By clearly defining your limits and asserting them when necessary, you create boundaries that safeguard your well-being. These boundaries allow you to conserve your energy, set aside time for self-care, and maintain a healthy balance in your life. As a result, you experience greater emotional resilience, inner peace, and a deeper sense of equilibrium, even amid life's challenges and stressors.

Authentic living: Setting healthy boundaries is synonymous with living authentically. It's about honoring your truth and living in alignment with your values, desires, and needs. When you assert your boundaries, you assert your right to be yourself unapologetically. You refuse to compromise your authenticity or betray your innermost beliefs for the sake of others' approval or acceptance. Instead, you prioritize your own well-being and honor your unique essence. By setting and maintaining boundaries that reflect who you truly are, you create the conditions for a life that is genuine, fulfilling, and deeply meaningful. In essence, asserting boundaries is an act of self-empowerment that liberates you to live your life on your own terms, in full alignment with your authentic self.

So, as you start down your own path of self-discovery and empowerment, remember that setting boundaries is not about being less nice. It's about being more authentically you. It's about embracing your power, harnessing your strength, and stepping boldly into the world as the strong, self-loving woman you are meant to be.

The Impact of Boundary Violations

The profound impact that boundary violations can have on our mental health, interpersonal relationships, and personal boundaries needs to be addressed. It's crucial to understand that when our boundaries are disregarded or violated, it triggers a cascade of effects that ripple through every aspect of our lives. Continuous boundary oversteps can exhaust an individual's coping mechanisms, making it more challenging to effectively handle daily stressors.

How Our Brain Reacts

When someone crosses our boundaries, our brain sees it as a danger to our safety. This makes us react with fight, flight, or freeze responses. Many are familiar with the fight-or-flight response, but the freeze response is less recognized. It comes into play when the brain determines that neither fighting nor fleeing can effectively handle the threat. When a freeze response is activated, a person might briefly feel immobilized or unable to respond. They could experience a sense of being trapped, powerless, or unable to react appropriately in that moment. People who have the habit of pleasing others often get stuck in the freeze response. They end up agreeing to everything, even if it's against what they want, just to avoid disagreements.

Choosing the freeze response keeps the cycle of boundary breaches going and harms our mental well-being. It slowly eats away at our self-value and self-esteem, making us feel weak and drained. This continual prioritization of others' needs can lead to increased levels of tension, worry, and (sometimes) sadness.

The problem with constantly prioritizing others' needs over our own is that it becomes a pattern. This pattern, if left unaddressed, can lead to a lack of self-identity and a diminished belief in our abilities. It can also make us neglect our own needs and emotions, building up a sense of frustration and resentment over time.

Interpersonal Dynamics

Boundary violations can wreak havoc on our interpersonal dynamics. Without clearly defined boundaries, you can struggle to assert yourself and communicate your needs effectively. This often leads to misunderstandings, resentment, and strained relationships; it can severely damage trust between people, making it difficult to maintain open and honest relationships. Others may inadvertently take advantage of your lack of boundaries, assuming that your kindness equates to permission to overstep your limits.

For those going through life without defined boundaries, self-expression can feel like an uphill battle. You may suppress your true thoughts and feelings out of fear of rejection or disapproval, sacrificing your authenticity in the process. This not only diminishes your sense of self but, also, hinders your ability to form genuine connections with others.

Types of Boundaries

When breaking free from the restrictions of nice girl syndrome, it's imperative to understand the multifaceted nature of boundaries and their profound impact on our well-being and relationships. Boundaries come in various forms, each serving a unique purpose in safeguarding our physical, emotional, and mental health. Let's explore the different types of boundaries and their relevance in our quest for genuine self-care and empowerment.

Physical Boundaries

Physical boundaries encompass the tangible space around us and dictate how close or distant we allow others to come into our personal space. This includes boundaries related to touch, personal belongings, and physical privacy. For example, setting physical boundaries might involve asserting your comfort level with hugging or maintaining personal space in crowded environments.

Imagine you're at a social gathering, and a friend of a friend approaches you. As they engage in conversation, you notice that they continuously invade your personal space, standing uncomfortably close, and placing a hand on your waist. The nice girl syndrome can make you feel trapped. Despite subtle cues, such as stepping back or adjusting your posture to create more distance, they persist in encroaching on your physical boundaries.

In this scenario, the individual is crossing a physical boundary by disregarding your need for personal space and invading your comfort zone. This intrusion can leave you feeling uneasy, anxious, or even violated as your sense of autonomy and safety is compromised.

Emotional Boundaries

Emotional boundaries revolve around protecting our emotions, feelings, and innermost thoughts. These boundaries govern how much emotional intimacy we share with others and how we respond to their emotions. Establishing emotional boundaries might entail recognizing and expressing your feelings openly, while also respecting the emotions of others without taking them on as your own.

Picture this: You're confiding in a close friend about a personal challenge you're facing at work. As you open up and share your feelings, your friend interrupts you with unsolicited advice, dismissing your emotions and invalidating your experience. Instead of offering empathetic support, they immediately jump into problem-solving mode, leaving you feeling unheard and invalidated. The nice girl in you smiles politely and nods.

In this scenario, the friend is crossing an emotional boundary by failing to respect your need for validation and empathetic listening. By offering unsolicited advice, instead of simply being present and validating your emotions, they undermine the trust and intimacy of the relationship.

Mental Boundaries

In our daily lives, mental boundaries are like protective shields around our thoughts, beliefs, and opinions. These boundaries are essential as they help us defend ourselves against unwanted thoughts, intellectual manipulation, and overwhelming cognitive burdens. They serve as barriers that safeguard our personal ideas, values, and opinions. Think of mental boundaries as invisible fences that define our individuality and dictate how we engage with the thoughts and opinions of others. These boundaries are crucial for maintaining a strong sense of self, especially when navigating environments with diverse viewpoints.

Having clear mental boundaries allows us to establish a sense of psychological security and autonomy. It empowers us to express our thoughts freely without feeling pressured to conform to external influences. For example, in a workplace setting, having strong mental boundaries can help us stay true to our principles and values when faced with conflicting opinions or demands. This ability to maintain one's personal convictions in the face of opposition or differing perspectives is a testament to the strength of our mental boundaries.

Healthy mental boundaries are integral to fostering a positive self-concept. By respecting our boundaries, we acknowledge and validate our inner beliefs and values. This self-awareness enables us to engage in meaningful interactions with others while staying true to ourselves. It allows us to appreciate the diversity of opinions and perspectives without compromising our own sense of identity. For instance, when engaging in discussions or debates, individuals with well-defined mental boundaries are better equipped to articulate their viewpoints confidently, contributing to constructive dialogue and mutual understanding.

Imagine you're engaging in a passionate discussion or a disrespectful disagreement with a colleague about a project at work. As you express your ideas and opinions, your colleague continually interrupts you, dismisses your perspectives, and attempts to impose why your beliefs are invalid and their viewpoints are superior. They are relentless in trying to convince you of this. Despite your attempts to assert your thoughts and maintain control over the conversation, they persist in dominating the discussion and disregarding your input.

In this scenario, the colleague is violating a mental boundary by disregarding your autonomy and attempting to impose their own beliefs and opinions onto you. By interrupting and dismissing your ideas, they undermine your ability to think independently and assert your own thoughts and perspectives.

Interpersonal Boundaries

Interpersonal boundaries govern the dynamics of our relationships with others, including family, friends, colleagues, and acquaintances. These boundaries dictate the level of closeness, communication, and emotional exchange we share with different individuals. They determine the amount of time and focus you are willing to invest in various relationships, as well as your expectations for how your time should be valued by others. Setting interpersonal boundaries might entail asserting your needs and preferences in relationships, communicating openly and assertively, and recognizing when to prioritize your own well-being. These boundaries are crucial for preserving healthy, respectful, and functional relationships in every aspect of life.

Envision this: You've made it clear to your romantic partner that you need some alone time to recharge after a long day at work. Despite your explicit request, your partner consistently disregards your need for space and constantly seeks your attention—whether it's through incessant texting, unexpected visits, or constant demands for your time and energy. They become upset or offended when you try to assert your boundaries, dismissing your need for space as unnecessary or unreasonable.

In this scenario, your partner is violating an interpersonal boundary by failing to respect your need for personal space and autonomy. By persistently intruding on your alone time and dismissing your boundaries, they undermine your sense of agency and create tension and resentment in the relationship.

Material Boundaries

Money has been a long-standing difficult and sensitive topic, especially among family and friends. Whether you're facing situations such as being invited to an event beyond your budget, refusing to lend money, or requesting repayment from a friend, it's important not to let feelings of guilt or shame take over. It's crucial to recognize that everyone, including you, has varying spending preferences, incomes, and financial limits, prompting the need to eliminate the awkwardness surrounding discussions about money.

Imagine you've set a budget for yourself and communicated it clearly to your family members. What is your goal? It's purchasing your first home. Despite your efforts to stick to your financial plan, a family member consistently asks you for loans or financial assistance without considering your budget constraints. They may guilt-trip you or pressure you into lending them money, even when you express reluctance or explain that it's not feasible for you at the moment.

In this scenario, the family member is violating a financial boundary by disregarding your budgetary limitations and repeatedly requesting financial support without considering your financial well-being. By pressuring you to lend them money, despite your reservations, they undermine your financial autonomy and create stress and strain in the relationship.

Material boundaries extend beyond finances, including possessions like cars, clothing, or maybe a vacation home. Whether you're facing a request to borrow money or lend out personal belongings, it's key to maintain boundaries that respect both your resources and your relationships.

Perhaps a friend asks to borrow your car for an extended period, or a sibling wants to use your vacation cabin for a weekend getaway. Just like with money, it's essential to set clear boundaries around lending out your possessions. While it's natural to want to help loved ones, it's equally important to prioritize your own needs and limitations.

When faced with requests for financial or material assistance, it's important to communicate your boundaries assertively and respectfully. Let your loved ones know what you're comfortable with and what you're not, and be firm in upholding those boundaries. Remember, setting boundaries isn't selfish—it's an act of self-care that ultimately strengthens your relationships and preserves your well-being.

Understanding the interconnectedness of these boundary types is key in fostering a holistic approach to boundary-setting. It helps ensure that self-care is balanced across all aspects of life. For example, maintaining strong physical boundaries can bolster our emotional resilience, while clear emotional boundaries contribute to healthier interpersonal dynamics. By honing our skills in navigating the spectrum of boundary types, we give the power back to ourselves to nurture relationships that are built on mutual respect, understanding, and authenticity. It establishes the groundwork for a harmonious, considerate, and fulfilling life.

As you reflect on the various types of boundaries, consider how each type manifests in your own life and relationships. What areas do you feel confident in asserting your boundaries, and where do you find yourself struggling?

Identifying Your Boundaries

Boundaries act as protectors of our well-being, directing us in asserting our requirements, principles, and boundaries with certainty and precision. How can we initiate the process of unraveling the complexities of our boundaries and re-establishing control over our personal space and autonomy? Let us look at several impactful strategies for recognizing your boundaries:

Self-reflection and introspection: Begin by carving out moments of stillness and solitude for self-reflection and introspection. Set aside time each day to connect with your innermost thoughts, feelings, and desires. You will find a journaling exercise at the end of this chapter. These can be powerful tools for exploring your values, needs, and limits.

Pay attention to your emotional responses: Our emotions serve as invaluable guides in identifying our boundaries. Pay close attention to the emotions that arise in various situations or interactions. Notice when you feel uneasy, resentful, or drained. For example, do you feel an increase in anxiety when someone violates your personal space? This is a clear indication that your personal boundaries need to be strengthened. These emotional cues can signal areas where your boundaries may be compromised or violated. Trust your intuition and honor your emotional responses as valuable indicators of your needs and limits.

Recognize triggers and warning signs: Take note of situations, behaviors, or interactions that consistently trigger discomfort or dissatisfaction within you. These triggers and warning signs can offer valuable insights into areas where your boundaries may be tested or overlooked. Whether it's feeling pressured to say *yes* when you want to say *no,* or enduring disrespectful treatment from others, recognizing these patterns empowers you to take proactive steps in asserting your boundaries. A perfect example of this is when someone asks to borrow money. Whether this is a close friend or family member, if you are struggling to say no, despite it being in your best interest, your financial boundary needs work.

Seek support and feedback: Don't hesitate to reach out to trusted friends, family members, or mentors for support and feedback as you move through the process of identifying your boundaries. Share your insights, reflections, and concerns with those who know and understand you best. Their perspectives and observations can offer invaluable validation and guidance as you strive to honor your truth and assert your boundaries with confidence.

When you are able to identify your boundaries, you reclaim ownership of your personal space and autonomy, paving the way for a life lived boldly and unapologetically. Trust yourself, honor your truth, and embrace the radiant authenticity that awaits you.

Distinguishing Healthy vs. Unhealthy Boundaries

Remember that understanding the nuances of boundaries is key to fostering relationships built on mutual respect and empowerment.

Healthy Boundaries

Healthy boundaries embody a harmonious and respectful approach to interpersonal connections, empowering us to honor our own needs while respecting those of others. Here are the hallmarks of healthy boundaries:

Self-awareness: Healthy boundaries begin with self-awareness, where we tune into our emotions, values, and limits. Recognizing our own needs and discomforts allows us to build the foundation for effective boundary-setting and communication.

Assertiveness: Assertiveness is essential to healthy boundaries, enabling us to express ourselves openly, honestly, and with respect. It involves advocating for our rights and needs while acknowledging and considering the boundaries of others.

Mutual respect: Healthy boundaries foster mutual respect within relationships, ensuring that both parties feel heard, acknowledged, and valued. This balanced dynamic honors individuality and encourages authentic connection without compromising personal integrity.

Emotional regulation: Maintaining healthy boundaries requires emotional regulation, where we skillfully manage our emotions and respond to them in constructive ways. By recognizing and expressing our feelings while respecting the emotions of others, we cultivate healthy, balanced relationships.

Unhealthy Boundaries

Conversely, unhealthy boundaries can lead to emotional turmoil, dependency, and strained connections. Here are the telltale signs of unhealthy boundaries:

Codependency: Unhealthy boundaries often manifest in codependent relationships, where people become overly reliant on each other for validation, identity, or decision-making. This dynamic erodes autonomy and neglects individual needs, perpetuating a cycle of dependency.

Enmeshment: Enmeshed boundaries blur our distinctions and personal space, fostering emotional fusion and control. This unhealthy intertwining of emotions can lead to a loss of autonomy and identity, as one person's feelings heavily influence the other's.

Emotional neglect: Weak boundaries may result in emotional neglect, where we prioritize others' needs at the expense of our own. This self-neglect breeds resentment, exhaustion, and a diminished sense of self-worth, ultimately undermining personal well-being.

Violation: Violating another's boundaries, whether consciously or unconsciously, fractures trust and inflicts emotional harm. This includes disregarding personal space, dismissing feelings, or engaging in manipulative behavior, thus eroding the foundation of healthy relationships.

Setting Boundaries Effectively

When you start down the path of breaking free from the confines of nice girl syndrome, setting boundaries effectively becomes key in genuine self-care and empowerment. Let's review a step-by-step guide to articulating boundaries with clarity, assertiveness, and respect.

Step 1: Self-Reflection and Clarity

Begin by tuning into your innermost thoughts, feelings, and needs. Take time to identify areas of your life where you feel discomfort, resentment, or overwhelm. Ask yourself:

- What are my core values, needs, and priorities?

- What specific behaviors or situations trigger negative emotions or discomfort

Step 2: Define Your Boundaries

Once you've gained clarity on your needs and limits, it's time to define your boundaries with precision and clarity. Be specific about what behaviors, actions, or interactions are acceptable and unacceptable to you. For example:

Step 3: Communicate Your Boundaries

In some cases, it may be necessary to set consequences for boundary violations. Be prepared to follow through on these consequences if the boundary is crossed. For example:

Setting boundaries can be challenging, especially if you're used to prioritizing others' needs over your own. Remember to be gentle with yourself and practice self-compassion throughout the process. It's okay to feel uncomfortable or anxious, but know that you are deserving of respect and consideration. This will get easier the more familiar it becomes to you.

By following these steps and embracing the art of setting boundaries effectively, you give yourself the power to live a life filled with comfort, self-respect, and genuine connection.

Mastering the art of communication becomes essential when establishing boundaries. Whether it's in personal relationships, work environments, or social settings—effective boundary communication lays the foundation for authentic connection, mutual respect, and empowered self-care. Let's explore some empowering techniques for communicating boundaries in different contexts:

While assertiveness is essential in setting boundaries, it's also important to approach boundary-setting with a spirit of collaboration and flexibility. Here are some strategies for negotiating boundaries collaboratively and seeking compromise when necessary:

You are deserving of self-respect and self-care, as well as understanding and support, in every aspect of your life. Keep embracing your boldness, keep saying *no* when needed, and keep communicating and negotiating those healthy boundaries.

As we continue our exploration of overcoming nice girl syndrome and embracing authentic self-care, the mastery of boundary enforcement emerges as a pivotal aspect. Upholding boundaries transcends mere restriction-setting; it epitomizes the assertion of self-worth, safeguarding personal well-being, and asserting the prerogative of self-respect and empowerment. Let's look into refined strategies for enforcing boundaries and discussing violations with unwavering composure and efficacy:

Trust in your capacity, uphold your inherent worth, and assert your entitlement to unfettered self-expression. Uphold your boundaries, and exude confidence in your convictions.

6

Finding Your Voice

You deserve to be heard. Your thoughts, feelings, and desires are valid, and it's time to reclaim ownership of your voice. In this chapter, we'll look closely into the art of communication, exploring how to assert yourself effectively and speak your truth with confidence.

Imagine a life where you no longer censor yourself, where you express your opinions openly, and where you advocate for your own well-being without guilt or hesitation. That life is within reach, and it starts with finding and embracing your unique voice.

Are you ready to step into your power? By the end of this chapter, you'll not only have honed your communication skills but also discovered the liberating joy of being authentically you. It is time to amplify your voice, unleash your inner boldness, and embrace a life filled with genuine self-care and empowerment. It's time to speak up, stand tall, and shine brightly.

What Is Assertive Communication

Have you ever found yourself struggling to express your thoughts clearly without feeling like you're being too pushy? Or, perhaps, you've encountered difficulty articulating your own needs?

Consider this common scenario: You're swamped with a looming deadline for a crucial project, and your friend reaches out, urgently asking for a favor. You want to maintain your focus, yet you hesitate, fearing you'll be labeled as a bad friend if you decline.

Can you relate? How can we remedy these situations? Assertive communication is a powerful tool in breaking free from the confines of niceness. Assertive communication empowers you to uphold your rights and boundaries while respecting those of others.

At its core, it's about confidently expressing your needs in a manner that is both firm and respectful. It's finding the middle ground between passivity and aggression, standing up for yourself without bulldozing over others.

For example, calmly state your boundaries to your friend, acknowledging their request while also prioritizing your own commitments. This approach not only fosters healthier relationships but also alleviates the guilt that often accompanies saying *no* when necessary.

Assertive communication is a skill that transcends contexts—it's indispensable in the workplace, within friendships, and even in family dynamics. It is the key to healthy interpersonal relationships and effective conflict resolution. It empowers you to voice your opinions, advocate for your needs, and, ultimately, foster genuine self-care.

The Difference Between Assertive, Passive, and Aggressive Communication

Let's revisit the scenario we discussed earlier. Your friend requests a last-minute favor while you're engrossed in an important project. How do you respond?

An aggressive approach might involve snapping back with frustration, placing blame, and dismissing your friend's needs entirely. This response risks damaging your relationship and escalating tension.

On the flip side, a passive response involves brushing aside your own priorities to accommodate others, often at the expense of your own well-being. While it may seem easier in the moment, it ultimately undermines your self-respect and can lead to resentment.

Now, consider the assertive response—a balanced blend of confidence and empathy. By politely declining the request and expressing your current commitments, you uphold your boundaries without belittling your friend. This approach honors both your needs and theirs, fostering mutual understanding and respect.

Picture yourself calmly asserting your boundaries, recognizing your worth, and advocating for your priorities with grace and clarity. This embodies assertive communication, a fundamental aspect needed for freeing oneself from nice girl syndrome.

Let us further explore these unique communication styles (Gatchpazian, n.d.):

Passive	Assertive	Aggressive
Hesitant to express opinions	Speaks plainly and assuredly	Speaks with aggravation or anger
Won't look others in the eyes	Looks someone directly in the eyes	Stares critically or judgmentally
Struggles to decline requests or demands	Capable of calmly and directly refusing	Refuses in an aggressive or reactive manner
Places others' needs above own	Considers both self and others' needs	Places own needs above others'
Adopts a small or slouched posture	Maintains a firm, comfortable posture	Displays closed or expansive posture
Diminishes own self-esteem	Boosts own self-esteem	Diminishes others' self-esteem
Speaks in a soft or weak tone	Speaks in a firm manner	Speaks loudly or forcefully, potentially shouting
Seeks to please others	Seeks to express personal needs	Seeks to dominate or overpower

Reflect on your own communication patterns. Do you tend to lean toward passivity, aggression, or assertiveness? Perhaps you find yourself oscillating between different styles, depending on the situation.

Research shows that assertive communication is the most effective across multiple situations. It upholds self-respect and respect for others—fostering honesty, clarity, and constructive communication that can be advantageous in numerous settings, ranging from personal to professional relationships. (Gatchpazian, n.d.).

How to Develop Assertiveness Skills and Integrate Them Into Daily Life

Maybe you struggle to assert yourself in various scenarios? Others you know may be assertive in some contexts, but not in others. It is essential to bear in mind that the ability to be assertive is a skill that can be developed like any other—with deliberate practice and strategic planning. Assertive communication not only improves interpersonal relationships but, also, upholds personal integrity and self-respect.

In everyday situations, passive communication can pose challenges when our needs go unfulfilled consistently. This may result in anxiety, frustration, diminished self-worth, and potential conflicts in significant relationships.

Here are five top tips on increasing assertive communication:

Be clear when defining goals: One common challenge is not having a clear understanding of your goals or the messages you want to convey. Taking time to define your goals can increase the chances of meeting your needs. It's important to be specific when defining your goals.

Be strategic: In general, people are more receptive to assertive communication when they are not fatigued, stressed, or distressed. Opt for a time and setting characterized by tranquility and minimal disruptions for effective interaction. Simply put, it's about picking the right moment and time.

Identify and challenge: Negative thoughts regarding our assertiveness and its potential outcomes can hinder our ability to assert ourselves effectively. To overcome these obstacles, consider how you would advise a friend facing similar thoughts or draw upon your past experiences with assertiveness to counter any negative assumptions.

Develop an assertiveness script and rehearse it: Effective communication involves preparation, especially in emotional situations. Write down your message before the discussion to stay focused. Practice in front of a mirror or with a friend to improve your delivery.

Utilize the broken record technique: When we're sharing information or ideas that might be new or contrary to common beliefs, it can often take time before they start to resonate with others. This is where the "broken record" technique comes into play. It's a simple yet powerful method to make sure your message sticks.

Techniques for Effective Communication

Finding your voice is essential for nurturing healthy relationships and personal growth. Let's explore essential techniques to enhance your communication skills and truly amplify your unique voice in interactions:

Clear expression of thoughts and feelings: Articulating yourself clearly and assertively is fundamental for effective communication. Utilizing "I" statements enables you to express thoughts and emotions without adopting a defensive or accusatory tone. For instance, rather than stating, "You consistently overlook my contributions," you might express, "I feel undervalued when my contributions are not acknowledged." Taking ownership of your experiences, you promote transparent dialogue and mutual comprehension.

Avoid excessive apologizing: While offering apologies when warranted is important, excessive apologizing can undermine your confidence and assertiveness. Strive to maintain a balanced approach, reserving apologies for genuine mistakes or offenses. Asserting your needs or boundaries without undue apology demonstrates self-assurance and promotes assertiveness in communication.

Active listening: Active listening signals respect and fosters meaningful connections. Dedicate your attention to the speaker without interjecting, and employ techniques such as paraphrasing or summarizing to demonstrate comprehension. Non-verbal cues, such as attentive nodding and consistent eye contact, convey engagement and facilitate open dialogue. By practicing active listening, you cultivate trust and cultivate an environment conducive to productive discourse.

Clarity and conciseness: Communication clarity and conciseness are pivotal in ensuring message comprehension. Strive to communicate in straightforward language, avoiding excessive jargon or convoluted expressions that may obscure meaning. Keep your communication succinct and focused, particularly when asserting boundaries or expressing needs. Clear, concise communication minimizes the risk of misinterpretation and fosters effective exchanges.

Non-verbal communication: Non-verbal cues—including body language, facial expressions, and tone of voice—significantly influence communication dynamics. Consistently align your non-verbal signals with your verbal message to convey sincerity, openness, and professionalism. Mindful use of non-verbal communication enhances message impact and facilitates rapport-building. By leveraging non-verbal cues effectively, you project confidence and credibility in your interactions.

Conflict resolution skills: Conflict resolution proficiency is indispensable for navigating interpersonal challenges constructively. Approach conflicts with a collaborative mindset, prioritizing resolution over contention. Employ strategies such as compromise, collaboration, and negotiation to foster mutually beneficial outcomes. Avoid adversarial approaches and, instead, focus on understanding diverse perspectives and facilitating consensus. By adeptly managing conflicts, you foster a culture of respect and cooperation within your interpersonal relationships.

Integrate these professional communication techniques into your repertoire and you will enhance your ability to communicate effectively, cultivate professional relationships, and handle challenges with composure and professionalism. Recognize communication as a continuous refinement process, and embrace opportunities for growth and development in your communication endeavors.

Overcoming Fear of Conflict

Do you often compromise your opinions to avoid disagreement? We are socialized to prioritize harmony, which can lead to a fear of conflict, making us more likely to compromise our opinions to avoid disagreement. This can ultimately impact your ability to find your voice and assert your opinions confidently in various situations.

However, freedom from this pattern begins with a comprehensive understanding and appreciation of the constructive potential inherent in conflict. It's a gateway to better understanding, creative problem-solving, and improved relationships, if managed effectively. Contrary to popular belief, conflict—when managed adeptly—can also fortify relationships and lead to self-care.

In the following steps, we'll explore practical strategies to help you overcome fear of conflict with courage and conviction, so you can find your voice and advocate for yourself with confidence:

Step one—Understand the root of your fear: The initial stride toward overcoming the fear of conflict necessitates introspection to discern its origins. Reflect on past encounters; is there a recurrent theme of adverse consequences stemming from conflict? Are concerns regarding rejection or social censure prevalent? By pinpointing these underlying factors, one can commence the process of dismantling their influence.

Step two—Reframe your perspective: Having gained insight into the origins of your conflict aversion, the next imperative is to reframe your perception of conflict. Transition from viewing it as a threat to embracing it as an opportunity for constructive dialogue and resolution. Acknowledge that healthy conflict is an integral facet of interpersonal dynamics, both in personal and professional realms.

Step three—Embrace growth mindset: Avoiding conflict merely defers its resolution and stifles personal development. Embrace the discomfort inherent in confronting conflict, recognizing that it serves as a conduit for personal evolution and relational depth.

Step four—Hone effective communication skills: Mastering conflict resolution demands proficiency in communication. Cultivate active listening, empathy, and assertiveness. Articulate your viewpoints with clarity and conviction, while remaining receptive to alternative perspectives. Understand that conflict resolution is a collaborative endeavor, driven by mutual understanding and respect.

Step five—Practice self-compassion: Extend compassion to yourself throughout this journey. Recognize that progress is incremental and celebrate each milestone, irrespective of magnitude. Treat yourself with the same kindness and understanding you afford others facing similar challenges.

When you acknowledge conflict not as a hindrance but as a conduit for personal growth and authenticity, you reclaim agency over your narrative, emancipate yourself from the constraints of niceness, and find your voice.

Strategies for Overcoming Fear of Conflict

View conflict as an opportunity for personal development and self-empowerment. Embrace your worth, assert your boundaries, and advocate for your needs confidently. You are deserving, capable, and equipped to lead a life aligned with your values and aspirations.

Understanding the fear of conflict: The fear of conflict is deeply ingrained in women suffering from nice girl syndrome. Yet, conflict is an inevitable aspect of life, providing opportunities to assert boundaries, express needs, and advocate for oneself.

Managing emotions: Effectively managing emotions is pivotal in moving through confrontational situations. While it's natural for emotions to intensify in such scenarios, allowing them to dictate our responses can lead to detrimental outcomes. Implementing mindfulness techniques, such as controlled breathing or grounding exercises, can help maintain composure and clarity in challenging moments.

Building confidence: Confidence is key in confronting conflict with poise and assertiveness. Begin by acknowledging your inherent value and strengths as a strong woman. Reflect on past accomplishments and positive attributes to foster a resilient self-image. Incrementally challenge yourself to address conflicts, setting achievable goals that gradually expand your comfort zone. With each successful interaction, confidence in your ability to handle conflict will grow.

Setting boundaries: Establishing and upholding boundaries is essential for fostering healthy relationships and self-respect. Identify your non-negotiables and communicate them assertively and transparently. Practice asserting boundaries without guilt or apology when they are breached. Remember, prioritizing your own well-being is a fundamental right.

Throughout this guide, we've emphasized the necessity of reshaping both mindset and behavior to break free from the confines of nice girl syndrome. When you work to overcome the fear of conflict, you take another significant stride toward reclaiming personal agency, embracing authenticity, and prioritizing self-care.

Dealing With Backlash

Handling the change from accommodating to assertive can often invite pushback from those accustomed to the old you. Here's a strategic approach to managing backlash with poise and confidence:

Understanding Backlash

- Asserting your boundaries and needs can disrupt established dynamics, leading to varied reactions from others. From subtle dismissals to overt resistance, it's key to recognize and address these responses constructively. Moreover, manipulation tactics, like guilt-tripping, may be employed to dissuade you from asserting yourself.

Strategies for Dealing With Backlash

Maintain composure: In the face of criticism or hostility, prioritize maintaining a composed demeanor. Respond thoughtfully, rather than reacting impulsively, as composed reactions foster constructive dialogue.

Establish firm boundaries: Clearly articulate your boundaries and expectations with assertiveness and respect. Reinforce that your self-advocacy is non-negotiable, fostering mutual understanding and respect in your interactions.

Identify manipulative tactics: Be vigilant for guilt-tripping or manipulation attempts aimed at undermining your assertiveness. Recognize these behaviors and refuse to yield to them, maintaining your stance with confidence and conviction.

Coping Mechanisms for Handling Backlash

Self-reflection: Engage in introspection to process your emotions and reactions to backlash. Journaling or seeking guidance from a trusted confidant can aid in gaining clarity and perspective.

Practice self-compassion: Extend kindness and understanding to yourself during the challenges of asserting your boundaries. Embrace self-compassion as you navigate pushback, recognizing your inherent worth and resilience.

Seek support: Surround yourself with a supportive network of allies who champion your journey toward assertiveness. Draw strength from their encouragement and validation as you navigate obstacles along the way.

Professional assistance: If managing backlash becomes overwhelming or triggers deeper emotional turmoil, consider seeking professional guidance. Therapeutic support can equip you with coping mechanisms and insights to navigate interpersonal challenges effectively.

Embracing your authentic self requires courage and resilience. Confronting backlash with grace and determination will help you reclaim your agency and pave the way for a life guided by genuine self-care and fulfillment. Stay steadfast in your pursuit of authenticity, knowing that every step forward brings you closer to realizing your true potential.

✦ Exercise ✦

Exercise: Practicing Assertiveness in Different Contexts

Assertiveness is a skill that empowers you to express your thoughts, feelings, and needs confidently, while respecting the rights of others. It's about finding the balance between being too passive and too aggressive. As you continue to break up with niceness, let's explore exercises to practice assertiveness in various contexts. Let's focus on two important areas: assertive communication at *work* and assertive communication in *personal relationships*.

Assertive Communication at Work

Practice saying *no*: In your journal, write down any tasks or requests at work that you find overwhelming or that don't align with your priorities.

Instead of automatically saying *yes*, practice saying *no* assertively. Be clear, concise, and respectful in your response. For example, "I appreciate the opportunity, but my plate is full right now. Can we revisit this at a later time?" Using any of the examples above, how could you write your response?

Expressing your ideas: In meetings or brainstorming sessions, don't hesitate to share your thoughts and ideas. Practice speaking up confidently, even if your idea differs from others. Use "I" statements to express your viewpoints without sounding confrontational. For instance, "I believe there might be a more efficient approach we could explore."

Setting boundaries: Establish clear boundaries around your time and workload. Communicate your availability and limitations openly with your colleagues or supervisors. If you're feeling overwhelmed, don't hesitate to speak up and renegotiate deadlines or responsibilities. Write down an example of what you might say.

Assertive Communication in Personal Relationships

Expressing your feelings: Practice expressing your emotions openly and honestly with your loved ones. Use assertive communication to share your feelings without blaming or accusing others. For example, "I feel hurt when you cancel our plans without giving me notice. In the future, I'd appreciate it if you could communicate with me sooner."

Setting personal boundaries: Write down areas where you need to establish boundaries in your personal relationships. Whether it's with friends, family, or romantic partners, be clear about your limits and what you're comfortable with.

Practice saying *no* when necessary and assertively communicate your boundaries.

Handling conflict: Conflict is a natural part of any relationship. Practice assertive communication techniques to address conflicts constructively. Focus on finding solutions, rather than escalating the situation. Use active listening and empathy to understand the other person's perspective while, also, advocating for your own needs.

Remember, practicing assertiveness takes time and effort. Be patient with yourself as you develop this skill. Celebrate your progress along the way, and don't be afraid to seek support from a mentor, coach, or therapist if needed. By mastering assertive communication, you'll empower yourself to navigate both your professional and personal life with confidence and authenticity.

7

Self-Discovery and Embracing Authenticity

The journey of self-discovery and embracing authenticity is not about finding a fixed, unchanging self but, rather, about continually adapting and growing while maintaining alignment with core values and personal truths.

You may have found yourself agreeing to the desires of others while neglecting your own aspirations, or perhaps suppressing your emotions behind a facade of perpetual positivity.

The goal of this chapter is to lead you back to the unadulterated essence of your being: the authentic you.

Accepting authenticity entails more than mere self-expression; it involves honoring your values, boundaries, and aspirations without seeking external validation. It's about reclaiming agency over your life, aligning your actions with your core beliefs, and living in congruence with your true self.

Throughout this chapter, we'll uncover the intricacies of authenticity, address the barriers that impede its embrace, and find the path to freedom and empowerment.

The Importance of Authenticity

When we talk about authenticity, we're talking about more than just being honest or genuine; it's about living in alignment with who you truly are at your core. It's the act of being true to one's own personality, spirit, or character. It means letting go of the need to constantly please others or conform to societal expectations and, instead, embracing your own truth—even if it means being different or going against the grain.

Think of authenticity as the foundation upon which you build your life. When you're authentic, you're more likely to make choices that are in line with your values, leading to a greater sense of purpose and fulfillment. You're also better equipped to handle what life throws at you with resilience because you're grounded in your own truth.

Being authentic additionally fosters deeper and more meaningful connections with others. When you show up as your true self, you invite others to do the same, creating genuine bonds built on mutual respect and understanding.

Embracing authenticity isn't always easy, especially if you've spent years playing the role of the nice girl or trying to fit into a mold that isn't truly you. It requires courage and vulnerability to peel back the layers and reveal your authentic self to the world. However, the rewards far outweigh the discomfort.

When you embrace authenticity, you give yourself permission to live a life that is uniquely yours—a life that reflects your passions, dreams, and values. You become the author of your own story, empowered to create the kind of life you truly desire.

Research consistently shows that living authentically is not just a feel-good concept; it's a powerful catalyst for greater psychological well-being and satisfaction with life (Sutton, 2020). Let's uncover why embracing authenticity is key for your overall happiness and fulfillment:

Psychological well-being: Numerous studies have found a strong correlation between authenticity and psychological well-being. When you live authentically, you experience less internal conflict and greater congruence between your inner thoughts, feelings, and outward actions. This alignment leads to reduced stress, anxiety, and depression, and an overall greater sense of contentment and happiness in life (Sutton, 2020).

Attracts like-minded people: When you embody authenticity, you naturally draw in individuals who value and connect with your genuine self. This aids in establishing a compassionate and supportive social circle. Moreover, staying true to yourself enhances decision-making by illuminating your genuine desires and core values. This clarity enables you to make decisions aligned with your aspirations and principles.

Self-acceptance and inner peace: One of the most significant gifts of authenticity is the deep sense of self-acceptance and inner peace that comes with being true to yourself. Instead of constantly striving to meet others' expectations or fit into a mold that doesn't feel right, you learn to embrace your flaws, quirks, and imperfections as integral parts of who you are. This self-acceptance allows you to let go of self-judgment and foster a profound sense of inner peace and contentment.

Trust and deeper connections: People are naturally drawn to authenticity because it fosters genuine intimacy and allows for meaningful, heart-to-heart connections that transcend superficial interactions.

Pursuing passions and fulfilling potential: Living authentically empowers you to pursue your passions and fulfill your potential in life. When you're aligned with your true self, you're more attuned to your deepest desires, values, and interests. This clarity enables you to set meaningful goals, take purposeful action, and step into your full potential with confidence and conviction. Whether it's pursuing a career that aligns with your passions or cultivating hobbies that bring you joy, authenticity empowers you to live a life that is truly yours.

In essence, embracing authenticity isn't just about being true to yourself; it's about unlocking your full potential and living a life of genuine fulfillment and purpose.

How Authenticity Builds Resilience and Fosters Self-Confidence

Authenticity serves as a potent catalyst for bolstering resilience, equipping you with the fortitude to map out life's challenges with composure and strength. Embracing their authentic selves helps individuals build a more solid sense of self-assuredness for facing life's obstacles and a heightened sense of self-confidence. Let's take a closer look at the benefits of an authentic life:

Self-awareness: At the core of authenticity lies self-awareness: the capacity to discern and comprehend one's innermost thoughts, emotions, and motivations with impartiality. Embracing authenticity fosters a heightened sense of self-awareness, enabling people to discern their authentic desires, values, and boundaries. This self-awareness becomes the bedrock upon which strength is built, allowing you to confront adversities with clarity and authenticity. A realistic self-assessment helps avoid overwhelming situations that can occur due to overcommitment or underestimating challenges.

Fostering self-acceptance: Authenticity is synonymous with self-acceptance: an unconditional embrace of one's strengths, weaknesses, and imperfections. By embracing authenticity, you free yourself from the weight of societal expectations, loving yourself authentically. This radical self-acceptance strengthens resilience, instilling inner strength and conviction in the face of challenges. You recognize you inherent worthiness, independent of external validation, building strength anchored in self-acceptance.

Nurturing self-confidence: Embracing authenticity engenders profound self-confidence: the unwavering belief in one's worthiness and capabilities. Living authentically allows you to trust your instincts and judgment, confident in your expertise of your own life. Armed with this self-assurance, you confront challenges with resolve and assurance, rather than succumbing to self-doubt or insecurity. Authenticity builds strength by allowing you to confront adversity with authenticity and adaptability.

Handling Challenges: Authenticity equips you with the requisite tools to confront life's hurdles with flexibility and poise. Grounded in authenticity, you approach obstacles with a blend of genuineness, strength, and adaptability, eschewing resistance or avoidance. Adversities are embraced as opportunities for growth and refinement, underpinned by the belief that authenticity is the ultimate strength in overcoming challenges. Whether contending with setbacks, interpersonal conflicts, or tumultuous circumstances, authenticity enables you to emerge from adversity fortified and flexible.

Embracing authenticity becomes imperative when we want to break free from nice girl syndrome, paving the way for genuine self-care and empowerment.

Celebrating Uniqueness: Letting Go of External Validation

Do you ever find yourself constantly seeking approval from others, hoping it will make you feel better about yourself? It's a common struggle many of us face, but relying on external validation can lead to more harm than good.

When we tie our self-worth to the recognition and approval of others, we lose sight of our own value and strength. It's like we're living our lives on someone else's terms, constantly seeking validation just to feel accepted. But if we base our worth solely on how others perceive us, we're setting ourselves up for disappointment.

The truth is, no amount of external validation can fill the void within us. Consider the following:

- Seeking external validation can have a profound impact on our self-esteem. When we constantly look to others for approval, we begin to doubt our own worth. Over time, this reliance on external recognition can erode our sense of self and leave us feeling anxious and insecure.

- As we strive to please others, we often forget about our own value. Our worth becomes tied to how others perceive us, leading to a dangerous cycle of seeking validation. But the truth is, *our* opinion of ourselves matters most. We must reclaim our sense of self-worth and remember that we are valuable, regardless of others' opinions.

- The constant need for validation can take a toll on both our physical and emotional well-being. We devote endless time and energy to seeking approval, only to find ourselves feeling inadequate when it's not forthcoming. It's a draining cycle that leaves us feeling exhausted and unfulfilled.

- When we rely too heavily on external validation, we may become resentful toward those who don't validate us. We blame others for our lack of validation or success, which only serves to perpetuate feelings of bitterness. It's important to focus on our own internal sense of self-worth and not become consumed by resentment toward others.

- Chasing validation prevents us from reaching our full potential. When we prioritize others' opinions over our own desires and dreams, we limit ourselves. Comparison becomes our enemy, as we measure our worth against others' success. But true fulfillment comes from embracing our uniqueness and pursuing our own path.

We can break free from this cycle by recognizing that our worth isn't determined by the opinions of others. We are inherently valuable, regardless of whether or not others see it. By shifting our focus inward and learning to validate ourselves, we reclaim our power and confidence.

Sure, it's important to consider feedback from others but, ultimately, it's our own opinion of ourselves that matters most. *We* are the only ones who can truly define our worth, success, and capabilities. So why let someone else's opinion hold us back from being our authentic selves?

Chasing validation is not only exhausting, but it also robs us of the opportunity to reach our full potential. When we're constantly seeking approval, we may find ourselves making decisions that don't align with our true desires and dreams. We become so fixated on being accepted that we forget to prioritize our own goals and aspirations.

Instead of living a life of comparison, let's celebrate our uniqueness and embrace our individuality. We are all living our own life, and there's no one-size-fits-all definition of success. By letting go of the need for external validation, we open ourselves up to endless possibilities and opportunities for growth.

Relatable Examples

Let us explore the ways in which embracing individuality can grow a more fulfilling and authentic life:

Authentic connections: When we embrace our uniqueness, we attract people who accept us for who we truly are. Instead of trying to fit into molds that don't align with our authentic selves, we grow genuine connections with others who appreciate us for our quirks, strengths, and imperfections. These relationships are built on mutual respect and understanding, fostering a sense of belonging and support.

- **Example:** Suzanne used to suppress her love for art because she feared it wasn't "practical" enough. But when she embraced her passion and started sharing her creations with others, she found a community of like-minded people who celebrated her artistic talent. Now, she has deep connections with fellow artists who inspire and uplift her.

Personal fulfillment: Embracing our individuality allows us to pursue our passions and interests without reservation. When we prioritize our own happiness and fulfillment, we experience a profound sense of satisfaction and purpose. Whether it's pursuing a creative endeavor, exploring a new hobby, or following a career path that aligns with our values—embracing our uniqueness empowers us to live authentically and passionately.

Example: Maya always felt pressured to pursue a career in finance, following in her family's footsteps. However, she realized her true passion lay in environmental activism. Despite initial resistance from her loved ones, Maya followed her heart and dedicated herself to advocating for sustainability. Today, she feels fulfilled knowing she's making a positive impact on the world.

Self-confidence: Embracing our individuality boosts our self-confidence and self-esteem. When we fully accept ourselves for who we are, we radiate authenticity and inner strength. We no longer seek validation from external sources because we know our worth comes from within. This self-assurance empowers us to set boundaries, speak our truth, and pursue our goals with unwavering conviction.

Example: Emily struggled with body image issues for years, constantly comparing herself to unrealistic beauty standards. But when she embraced her unique features and celebrated her body for its strength and resilience, she gained a newfound confidence. Now, she walks with her head held high, unapologetically embracing her individuality and inspiring others to do the same.

Creative expression: Embracing our individuality unlocks our creativity and allows us to express ourselves freely. Whether it's through art, writing, music, or any other form of creative expression—we tap into our innermost thoughts, emotions, and experiences. This creative outlet serves as a powerful means of self-discovery and self-expression, enriching our lives and connecting us to our true essence.

Example: Julia always felt stifled in her corporate job, yearning for a creative outlet to express herself. So, she started a blog where she shared her personal stories, insights, and musings with the world. Through writing, Julia discovered her unique voice and connected with readers who resonated with her authenticity. Today, she feels alive and fulfilled, using her creativity to inspire and uplift others.

Empowerment and resilience: Embracing our individuality empowers us to overcome adversity and embrace life's challenges with flexibility. When we trust in our own abilities and stay true to ourselves, we handle obstacles with courage and determination. Our unique strengths and perspectives become sources of empowerment, guiding us through life's ups and downs.

Example: Rebecca faced criticism and judgment from others when she decided to pursue her dream of starting her own business. But she refused to let external opinions dim her light, trusting in her vision and capabilities. Despite setbacks and obstacles, Rebecca persevered, harnessing her strength and determination to turn her dream into reality. Today, she stands proud as a successful entrepreneur, proving that embracing individuality is the key to empowerment.

Self-Validation

Are you weary of the constant pursuit of external validation, perpetually seeking affirmation from others? It's time to free yourself from this cycle and honor your uniqueness. Let's uncover the path to authentic self-care by discovering the power of self-validation.

Understanding Self-Validation

Self-validation is the profound act of acknowledging and appreciating one's intrinsic worth and achievements without reliance on external sources. It entails embracing your truth, encompassing your idiosyncrasies, and traversing your personal journey with unwavering confidence and self-assurance.

Strategies for fostering self-validation:

Cultivate self-compassion: Extend to yourself the same compassion and empathy you would offer others. Embrace imperfections and setbacks as part of the human experience, nurturing an inner dialogue steeped in kindness and understanding.

Recognize personal strengths: Take stock of your unique strengths, talents, and accomplishments. Whether it's your flexibility in surmounting obstacles, your creativity, or your capacity for profound empathy, celebrate the qualities that render you exceptional. Maintain a record of your achievements to reinforce a sense of self-worth.

Establish boundaries: Prioritize your emotional well-being by setting clear boundaries that honor your needs. Learn to assertively decline commitments or relationships that detract from your sense of self-worth. Surround yourself with those who uplift and empower you, releasing those who diminish your self-esteem.

Focus on internal growth: Redirect your attention from external validation to personal growth and self-improvement. Set meaningful goals aligned with your values and aspirations, celebrating the incremental progress you achieve. Authentic fulfillment emanates from internal validation, not external approval.

Trust your judgment: Regularly practice making decisions on your own and trusting your judgment helps build confidence in your ability to rely on your internal guidance system.

Linking Self-Validation to Self-Care

Self-validation is key to genuine self-care, signaling a profound commitment to prioritizing one's well-being and contentment. Cultivating self-validation allows you to emancipate yourself from external approval, embracing self-care as a radical act of self-love that nourishes your mind, body, and spirit. Self-validation enhances emotional awareness and literacy, essential for effective self-care. By comprehending and embracing your emotional conditions, you can precisely determine the self-care required in any situation.

As you start supporting authenticity and celebrating your uniqueness, remember that your worth transcends external validation. Accept your complexities, your strengths, and your vulnerabilities with conviction. You are inherently deserving of love, respect, and validation by virtue of your existence.

Continue to free yourself from the confines of external validation, embracing the radiant, authentic being that you are. With steadfast determination, you are destined for profound growth and fulfillment.

Navigating Challenges and Overcoming Obstacles

Life presents us with countless obstacles and fears, but it's how we tackle these challenges that defines our growth. Confronting fears, surpassing previous experiences, and transcending personal limits unlock our genuine potential and lead to success. Let's dive into strategies to help you overcome these obstacles and fears, empowering you toward genuine self-discovery and fulfillment (Adams, 2023):

Celebrate your victories: When you overcome an obstacle or conquer a fear, take the time to acknowledge and celebrate your achievements. Recognizing your successes, no matter how small, can boost your self-confidence and reinforce the belief in your ability to overcome future challenges.

Develop a growth mindset: Support a growth mindset that sees challenges as opportunities for growth. Believe in your capacity to develop skills through dedication and effort. Every setback becomes a stepping stone to progress. Adopting a growth mindset makes you more resilient, better prepared to overcome your fears, and eager to embrace new opportunities.

Face your fears: To overcome fears, confront them! Challenge yourself to move away from what is comfortable and take risks. Though uncomfortable, pushing through these limitations leads to personal growth and newfound confidence.

Seek support and guidance: You don't have to face your fears and obstacles alone. Reach out to friends, family, mentors, or coaches for support and guidance. Sharing your challenges with others can help you gain new perspectives and insights, provide encouragement, and create a sense of accountability that can drive you to take action. Having someone in your corner can make all the difference, ensuring you thrive despite your fears.

Break down barriers into manageable steps: Confronting overwhelming challenges can be intimidating. Divide your obstacles into smaller, more manageable steps. Addressing them one by one helps you gain confidence and build momentum toward achieving your goals.

Own your limitations and fears: To begin conquering your fears you need to own their existence. It's essential to be honest with yourself about the barriers holding you back. Recognizing these hurdles allows you to create a roadmap to overcome them and propel yourself toward growth.

Techniques for Managing Fear and Self-Doubt

Managing fear and self-doubt is a pivotal aspect of breaking away from nice girl syndrome and fostering genuine self-care. Let's explore effective techniques tailored to empower you during the challenges and nurture unwavering confidence:

Mindfulness meditation: Mindfulness meditation stands as a potent practice for quieting the mind and enhancing self-awareness. Through regular sessions, you can nurture the ability to observe thoughts and emotions without judgment, fostering a deeper understanding of oneself. This heightened self-awareness enables you to confront challenges with clarity and composure.

Setting achievable goals: Break tasks into smaller steps. Establish small, achievable goals to avoid feeling overwhelmed, enhancing confidence as these goals are attained. Acknowledge small wins, such as recognizing and celebrating minor accomplishments that can generate momentum and reduce self-doubt.

Cognitive-behavioral strategies: Employing cognitive-behavioral strategies equips you with the means to challenge and replace negative thought patterns with constructive beliefs. When confronted with fear or self-doubt, it's imperative to scrutinize the underlying beliefs fueling these emotions. Ask probing questions: *Are these beliefs grounded in reality or assumption? How can I reframe these thoughts to foster empowerment?* Actively engaging in this process allows for a transformation of mindset, instilling greater confidence.

Self-affirmations: Utilizing self-affirmations entails regularly reinforcing positive beliefs about oneself. Commence each day by affirming personal strengths, capabilities, and worthiness. Consistent repetition of affirmations, such as "I possess confidence and competence," or "I trust in my capacity to surmount challenges," serves to counteract self-doubt and foster a mindset of assurance.

Challenging limiting beliefs: It is imperative to identify and challenge limiting beliefs hindering the full embrace of one's authentic self. Scrutinize beliefs such as "I am obliged to perpetually appease others" or "I am insufficient." Engage in a process of critical evaluation, seeking evidence to contradict these beliefs and reframing them in an empowering context.

Cultivating self-confidence: Building self-confidence is a gradual endeavor necessitating perseverance and acknowledgment of achievements, no matter how modest. Surround yourself with a supportive network and embrace opportunities for personal growth. Each step outside one's comfort zone contributes to the development of resilience and self-assurance.

Integrating mindfulness meditation, cognitive-behavioral strategies, and self-affirmations into your daily regimen allows you to effectively manage fear and self-doubt while fostering unwavering confidence. Accept this self-discovery and empowerment, recognizing your capacity to transcend nice girl syndrome and embody authenticity on your terms.

✦ Exercise ✦

Strength Spotlight: Journal Prompts Exercise

Take a moment to reflect on what truly matters to you. What principles guide your decisions and actions? In your journal, write down at least five core values that resonate deeply with you and explore why they are important.

Think about the activities or pursuits that light you up from within. What hobbies, interests, or causes ignite your enthusiasm? Jot down specific examples and reflect on how you can incorporate more of these passions into your life.

Reflect on any beliefs or narratives that may be holding you back from fully embracing your individuality. Write down what self-imposed limitations or negative thought patterns you need to release? Challenge yourself to reframe these beliefs with empowering alternatives.

Take stock of your unique strengths, talents, and qualities. Jot down what you are naturally good at. How do these strengths contribute to your sense of self-worth and purpose? Acknowledge and celebrate your gifts with gratitude.

Consider your personal boundaries in various areas of your life, such as relationships, work, and self-care. Write down what behaviors or situations you find unacceptable or draining. Clearly articulate your boundaries and explore ways to assert them firmly yet compassionately.

Self-Compassion Mindfulness Exercises

Body Scan Meditation

Find a comfortable seated or lying position and close your eyes. Bring your awareness to your breath, allowing it to anchor you in the present moment. Begin scanning your body from head to toe, noticing any sensations or areas of tension, without judgment. Take slow, deep breaths as you gradually release any physical or emotional tension you encounter.

Gratitude Practice

Take a few moments each day to cultivate gratitude for the present moment and the blessings in your life. Start a gratitude journal where you jot down three things you're thankful for each day. Whether it's a simple pleasure or a profound realization, focusing on gratitude can shift your perspective and foster a greater sense of contentment.

Mindful Movement

Engage in activities that allow you to connect with your body and the present moment, such as yoga or mindful walking. Pay attention to the sensations of movement, the rhythm of your breath, and the environment around you. Let go of distractions and immerse yourself fully in the experience.

Self-Compassion Meditation

Sit quietly and bring to mind a moment of struggle or difficulty you've experienced recently. Offer yourself words of kindness and understanding, acknowledging your humanity and inherent worth. Repeat compassionate phrases such as: "May I be kind to myself" or "May I embrace my imperfections with gentleness." Allow yourself to receive the warmth of self-compassion, without judgment.

Nature Connection

Spend time outdoors connecting with the natural world around you. Whether it's a walk in the park, a hike in the woods, or simply sitting beneath a tree—immerse yourself in the sights, sounds, and sensations of nature. Allow yourself to be present and receptive to the beauty and tranquility that surrounds you.

8

Building Resilience and Confidence

Now, as we approach the final chapter of this empowering guide, it's time to fortify ourselves with the essential tools of resilience and confidence. Forging ahead in the face of challenges requires a steadfast belief in oneself and the unwavering determination to overcome obstacles.

We'll discover the art of resilience: the ability to bounce back stronger and more resilient after setbacks. But resilience doesn't exist in isolation; it's intimately intertwined with confidence. True confidence isn't about arrogance or bravado; it's about owning your worth, standing tall in your convictions, and embracing your inherent power.

Throughout this chapter, you'll also have the opportunity to glean inspiration from the real-life stories of remarkable women who have triumphed over nice girl syndrome. Their stories serve as profound inspirations that confirm breaking free from the confines of niceness is not only possible but immensely rewarding.

The world is waiting for the bold, unstoppable force that you are destined to become. It is time to start this chapter with unwavering courage and boundless determination.

The Importance of Confidence and Resilience

Confidence, defined as the assured belief in yourself and your abilities, is integral to handling life's challenges and pursuing personal goals with determination. Resilience, meanwhile, denotes the capacity to rebound from setbacks and adversity, emerging stronger and more capable than before. Together, these qualities form the bedrock of personal development, empowering you to weather life's storms while maintaining a sense of purpose and self-assurance.

Confidence and resilience are like the dynamic duo of personal development. They work hand in hand to empower us to lead fulfilling, meaningful lives. Here's why they're so essential:

Empowerment: When you believe in yourself and your abilities, you're more likely to take risks, pursue your passions, and advocate for your needs. And when setbacks occur, as they inevitably will, resilience gives you the strength to dust yourself off and keep moving forward.

Self-Care: Genuine self-care is about nourishing your mind, body, and spirit in a holistic way. Confidence and resilience enable you to set boundaries, prioritize your well-being, and say *no* when necessary. They allow you to make choices that honor your needs and values, even when it's difficult.

Leadership: Whether you're leading a team at work, advocating for a cause you're passionate about, or simply leading by example in your everyday life—confidence and resilience are essential leadership qualities. They inspire others, they foster trust and respect, and they enable you to navigate uncertainty and change with poise and determination.

Healthy risk taking: Confidence promotes taking calculated risks that may result in substantial personal and professional development. Resilience guarantees that if risks do not unfold as anticipated, individuals can recover and make further attempts, gaining insight from their encounters.

For women, in particular, cultivating confidence and resilience is absolutely vital. Historically, women have been socialized to shrink themselves to fit into narrow societal expectations. But times are changing, and it's time for us to step into our power and reclaim our voices.

By developing confidence and resilience, women can:

Overcome limiting beliefs: Many women struggle with imposter syndrome: the feeling that they don't deserve their accomplishments and will be exposed as a fraud. Confidence helps women recognize their worth and internalize their successes, while resilience enables them to bounce back from setbacks and keep moving forward, despite any self-doubt.

Break up with niceness: True kindness and compassion start with oneself. By building confidence and resilience, women can set boundaries, advocate for their needs, and prioritize self-care without guilt or apology.

Being authentic: In a world that often expects women to conform to certain roles and expectations, confidence and resilience give women the power to lead with authenticity. They enable women to speak their truth, accept their uniqueness, and lead from a place of genuine integrity and purpose.

Strategies for Building Inner Strength and Confidence

Self-worth is the bedrock of our confidence and how we perceive ourselves in the world. It's the belief that you are inherently valuable and deserving of love, respect, and fulfillment simply because you exist. However, for many women—especially those affected by nice girl syndrome—self-worth can be elusive. Instead of recognizing your inherent value, you may seek validation and approval from others, constantly putting your own needs last.

When your self-worth is shaky, it's like building a house on sand. Your confidence becomes fragile and easily shaken by the opinions and actions of others. You may find yourself seeking external validation to feel good about yourself, relying on others to define your worth. This can lead to a cycle of people-pleasing, where you sacrifice your own needs and desires to maintain the illusion of being "nice."

Techniques for Recognizing and Appreciating Personal Value

Building inner strength and confidence hinges on recognizing and appreciating personal value. Through intentional practice and self-reflection, you can develop a deeper sense of personal value. Here are strategic techniques to guide you:

Reflect on accomplishments: Pause to acknowledge past achievements, whether significant milestones or everyday victories. Recognizing these successes reinforces a sense of capability and self-worth.

Identify unique qualities: Take inventory of your inherent qualities and attributes. Embrace your individuality, recognizing the value you bring to various aspects of your life and relationships.

Practice self-appreciation: Foster a habit of self-acknowledgment and gratitude. Maintain a journal to record personal strengths, positive traits, and aspects of life deserving appreciation.

Surround yourself **with positivity:** Foster a supportive environment by engaging with uplifting individuals, communities, and activities. Minimize exposure to negativity and criticism that may undermine self-esteem.

Challenge negative self-talk: Develop awareness of internal self-criticism and limiting beliefs. Counter negative thoughts with evidence of personal achievements and strengths, reinforcing a positive self-image.

Set and achieve goals: Establish meaningful objectives and pursue them with determination. Accomplishing goals contributes to a sense of competence and confidence in one's abilities.

Embrace self-compassion: Extend kindness and understanding to oneself, particularly in moments of difficulty or failure. Embrace imperfections with self-compassion rather than harsh judgment.

Practice mindfulness: Engage in mindfulness exercises to enhance self-awareness and present-moment focus. Mindfulness cultivates appreciation for oneself and fosters resilience in navigating life's challenges.

Exercises for Fostering Self-Compassion and Self-Acceptance

There are strategies for building inner strength and confidence designed to foster self-compassion and self-acceptance. These tools are critical in breaking away from being too nice and nurturing genuine self-care.

Embrace Your Reflection: The Mirror Exercise

Start by standing in front of a mirror, looking directly into your own eyes. This might feel uncomfortable at first, especially if you're not used to acknowledging yourself in this way. Take a few deep breaths and allow yourself to settle into the moment.

As you gaze at your reflection, affirm positive statements about yourself. Speak them aloud if you can. They can be simple affirmations like: "I am worthy," "I am enough," "I am strong," or "I am deserving of love and respect."

Notice any resistance or discomfort that arises and try to lean into it with compassion. Remember, this exercise is about embracing yourself fully, flaws and all. Over time, you'll find that the discomfort diminishes as your self-compassion grows.

Extend Forgiveness: The Letter to Self

Write a letter to yourself. Start by acknowledging any mistakes or perceived shortcomings you're holding onto. Be gentle with yourself as you reflect on these aspects of your life.

Next, write from a place of forgiveness, understanding, and empathy, recognizing that we are all imperfect beings on a path of growth. Release any guilt or shame you've been carrying and embrace the freedom that forgiveness brings.

Finally, affirm your commitment to self-love and acceptance. Remind yourself that you are worthy of forgiveness and deserving of compassion, just like anyone else.

Rephrase Your Inner Dialogue

Pay attention to the way you speak to yourself internally. Are you often critical or harsh? Challenge these negative thoughts by rephrasing them in a more compassionate and empowering way.

For example, if you catch yourself saying, "I'm such a failure," reframe it as, "I'm learning and growing from this experience." Instead of, "I'm not good enough," try saying, "I am constantly evolving into the best version of myself."

Practice replacing self-criticism with self-compassion whenever you notice negative thoughts creeping in. Over time, this shift in mindset will bolster your inner strength and confidence, empowering you to break free from the limitations of the nice girl syndrome.

Remember, building inner strength and confidence is a journey, not a destination. Be patient and kind to yourself along the way, celebrating every step forward, no matter how small. You deserve to live authentically and wholeheartedly, embracing your true self with love and compassion.

Understanding the Growth Mindset and Its Role in Resilience

Research on resilience indicates that those exhibiting a growth mindset, having faith in their ability to learn from errors and enhance their abilities, also foster greater resilience (*Embracing Resilience*, 2023).

Unlike a fixed mindset, which constrains us within the boundaries of perceived limitations, a growth mindset empowers us to confront challenges as avenues for growth and learning. This discourse aims to uncover the essence of the growth mindset, its profound impact on resilience and perseverance, and actionable strategies for its cultivation within ourselves and others.

The concept of a growth mindset stands as a counterpoint to its fixed counterpart. While a fixed mindset resigns those to the notion of static abilities, a growth mindset instills a proactive approach toward challenges, encouraging persistence in the face of adversity, and fostering a culture of acknowledging achievements, both personal and collective. It reframes setbacks not as reflections of inadequacy but as opportunities for personal development and progress.

A growth mindset equips you with the mental fortitude to handle life's trials, bounce back from setbacks, and pursue aspirations with unwavering determination. Perceiving challenges as catalysts for growth allows you to persist in the pursuit of goals despite obstacles. You can actively seek constructive feedback, building a resilience that propels you forward even during the most daunting circumstances.

Developing a growth mindset necessitates a deliberate and sustained effort. You must first identify and challenge fixed mindset tendencies, replacing them with constructive and realistic perspectives. Setting goals oriented toward continuous learning and improvement, and accepting feedback as a catalyst for growth, are key steps toward fostering a growth mindset.

As leaders, mentors, and influencers, it is incumbent upon us to foster environments that nurture growth mindsets in others. When we create cultures that prioritize learning and development, model vulnerability, and provide constructive feedback—we empower individuals to embrace challenges, foster growth, and unlock their full potential.

In the pursuit of professional and personal fulfillment, transcending the confines of niceness necessitates a steadfast commitment to fostering inner strength and confidence.

Strategies for Effective Goal-Setting and Planning

Are you ready to break free from the constraints of niceness and chart a course toward boldness and success? Let's take a closer look at discovering the power of setting effective goals, staying motivated, and overcoming obstacles with confidence and resilience.

Strategies for effective goal-setting and planning:

Write goals down: Take the first step toward achieving your dreams by putting pen to paper. Physically writing down your goals not only solidifies your intentions but also serves as a daily reminder of what you're striving for. Transform your aspirations into actionable steps, and watch as your vision comes to life.

Create SMART goals: SMART goals are your roadmap to success. By making your goals *Specific*, *Measurable*, *Achievable*, *Relevant*, and *Time-Bound*, you set yourself up for clarity and accountability. Break down your objectives into manageable tasks, ensuring that each step brings you closer to your ultimate vision (Damon, n.d.).

Set mini-goals: Sometimes, big dreams can feel overwhelming. Break them down into smaller, more manageable mini-goals. These bite-sized milestones not only keep you focused but also provide a sense of accomplishment along the way. Celebrate each small victory as you progress towards your larger goals.

Regularly review and adjust goals: Adaptability is critical. It is important to frequently reassess your goals to evaluate progress and make modifications according to new information or changes in circumstances. Flexibility is essential for remaining relevant and responsive to challenges.

Visualize success: Visualization is a powerful tool for goal achievement. Take a few moments each day to visualize yourself succeeding in your endeavors. Imagine how it will feel to accomplish your goals, and let that feeling fuel your motivation.

Tips for staying motivated and overcoming obstacles:

Find your why: Connect with the deeper purpose behind your goals. Why are they important to you? When you have a strong enough reason why, you'll be more motivated to persevere, even when faced with challenges.

Stay flexible: Life can get messy. Stay flexible and adapt your plans, as needed. Instead of seeing obstacles as roadblocks, view them as opportunities to learn and grow.

Stay positive: Positivity is key on the road to success. Foster a mindset of possibility and resilience, even in the face of challenges. Focus on solutions rather than dwelling on problems, and watch as your attitude propels you forward.

Build in accountability: Surround yourself with a support system that holds you accountable for your actions. Whether it's a mentor, coach, or accountability partner, having someone to share your goals with can keep you motivated and on track. Take ownership of your successes and failures, and let accountability drive you toward excellence.

Continuously evaluate progress: Progress isn't always linear, and that's okay. Continuously evaluate your journey, making adjustments as needed to stay aligned with your goals. Embrace the process of growth and learning, knowing that every challenge is an opportunity for improvement.

Dealing With Setbacks and Maintaining Assertiveness

Setbacks and disappointments are an inevitable part of life, but they don't have to derail us. Let's uncover how to handle these challenges while maintaining assertiveness and staying true to yourself.

First, it's important to recognize that setbacks and failures are not indicative of your worth or capabilities. They are simply detours on the road to success. Think of them as opportunities for growth and learning, rather than obstacles.

Setbacks often occur when we step out of our comfort zones or pursue ambitious goals. They can come in many forms, whether it's a rejection, a project that didn't go as planned, or a failed relationship. Understanding that setbacks are a natural part of life can help alleviate some of the sting when they occur.

Coping Mechanisms

Reframe the situation: Instead of viewing setbacks as failures, reframe them as opportunities for growth and learning. Ask yourself what lessons you can take away from the experience and how you can use it to become stronger and more resilient.

Maintain perspective: Zoom out and look at the bigger picture. One setback does not define your entire journey. Remind yourself of your past successes and the progress you've made. Keep your long-term goals in mind and stay focused on the bigger picture.

Take action: Rather than dwelling on what went wrong, channel your energy into productive action. Identify what steps you can take to move forward and regain momentum. Break down your goals into smaller, more manageable tasks and take proactive steps towards achieving them.

Practice assertiveness: Use setbacks as an opportunity to assert your needs and boundaries. If the setback was caused by external factors beyond your control, advocate for yourself and communicate your needs clearly. Assertiveness doesn't mean being aggressive; it means advocating for yourself with confidence and respect.

Don't take it personally: Stop indulging in self-pity. There are no benefits to feeling sorry for yourself. It's like poisoning yourself slowly; it affects you negatively.

Review, reflect, and readjust: No matter the circumstances, it is essential to analyze the situation, contemplate on it (*What occurred? What alternative actions could have been taken?*), and then make necessary adjustments. Alter your future behavior or responses accordingly.

Create an action plan: Ask yourself: *What is my next step?* If you're unsure, seek help, join a support group, or consider therapy. Take the necessary steps to create a plan to move ahead.

Stress and Anxiety

Recognizing and addressing the sources of stress and anxiety are critical for maintaining assertiveness and being resilient.

Identifying the sources of stress and anxiety:

Social expectations: As former "nice girls," we often internalize societal expectations to always be accommodating, nurturing, and agreeable. When we deviate from these norms, it can lead to feelings of guilt, fear of judgment, or rejection.

Perfectionism: The drive to please others can manifest as perfectionism, where we constantly strive for flawlessness in every aspect of our lives. This relentless pursuit of perfection can lead to immense pressure and anxiety when things don't go as planned.

Boundary challenges: Difficulty setting and maintaining boundaries is a hallmark of nice girl syndrome. Saying *no* or asserting our needs can trigger anxiety about disappointing others or being perceived as selfish.

Self-doubt: Years of prioritizing others' needs over our own can erode our self-confidence and foster self-doubt. We may question our worthiness, competence, or right to assert ourselves—leading to anxiety in assertive situations.

Coping strategies for managing stress and anxiety in challenging situations play a vital role in promoting emotional well-being, enhancing resilience, improving decision-making, preserving physical health, strengthening relationships, empowering self-advocacy, and fostering growth and development. Let's review those now:

Positive affirmations: Counteract self-doubt with positive affirmations that reinforce your worthiness and capabilities. Repeat affirmations such as "I deserve to prioritize my needs" or "I am capable of asserting myself respectfully" to boost your confidence and resilience.

Nature immersion: Spend time in nature to unwind and recharge. Engaging in activities such as hiking, gardening, or simply sitting in a park can have a calming effect on the mind and body, reducing stress levels and promoting relaxation.

Creative expression: Explore creative outlets like painting, writing, or playing music to channel stress into productive and fulfilling pursuits. Creative expression provides a healthy outlet for emotions, fosters self-expression, and promotes a sense of accomplishment and mastery.

Mindfulness practices: Incorporate mindfulness techniques such as meditation, deep breathing exercises, or body scans into your daily routine. Mindfulness fosters present-moment awareness, helps manage racing thoughts, and promotes a sense of calm and inner peace amidst life's challenges.

Physical activity: Engage in regular physical activity to release pent-up tension and boost mood-enhancing endorphins. Whether it's going for a run, practicing yoga, or dancing to your favorite music—exercise is a powerful antidote to stress, promoting physical health and mental well-being.

Gratitude journaling: Start a gratitude journal to focus on the positive aspects of life, even in difficult times. Each day, write down three things you're grateful for, no matter how small. Nurturing an attitude of gratitude shifts perspective, reduces stress, and enhances overall life satisfaction.

Inspiring Stories of Women Overcoming Nice Girl Syndrome

Marly's Story

Marly, a woman who proudly carried the reputation of the nice girl, was raised by parents who ingrained in her the virtues of politeness, selflessness, and prioritizing others above herself. Renowned for her willingness to assist others, she frequently put their needs ahead of her own, sometimes to her own detriment.

One day, Marly reached a breaking point. Balancing late nights at work, helping a friend move, and volunteering at a community event left her exhausted, overwhelmed, and out of touch with her own wants. That's when she acknowledged she was trapped by the nice girl syndrome.

Marly bravely chose to take back control of her life. She began by starting small, mastering the art of declining tasks that overwhelmed her, putting her needs first, and setting clear boundaries. It was challenging, and she encountered resistance and grappled with guilt. Nevertheless, she persevered, understanding that it was crucial for her personal development.

As Marly implemented these adjustments, her life went through a significant shift. She gained additional time for self-care, experienced a decrease in stress levels, and saw improvements in her relationships. People started to honor her boundaries and value her time—leading her to uncover a fresh sense of happiness, well-being, and confidence.

During her journey, Marly gained a significant insight: Practicing kindness doesn't entail overlooking oneself; rather, it involves achieving equilibrium. It's about understanding that it's acceptable to focus on our own needs, to decline when required, and to set boundaries that protect our welfare.

Marly discovered that with boundary-setting and self-prioritization, she can be kind, respectful, and empowered, without giving up on what makes her happy. It's about evolving from a people-pleaser to a self-advocate.

Charlotte's Story

Charlotte was a good girl from the start.

Raised to keep quiet, excel academically, and comply with authority—she absorbed the message that her voice mattered less, and her body and space were not entirely hers to control. Saying *no* wasn't encouraged; agreement was expected. Boundaries were foreign concepts. And prioritizing her own well-being often took a backseat to pleasing others.

For years, this facade served her well. She checked off all the boxes of what society deemed a good life. She got good grades, a respectable job, and a stable relationship. Yet, beneath the surface, she felt like an imposter in her own life, suffocating within the confines of others' expectations.

She couldn't ignore the growing sense of discontent within her—a longing for authenticity. So, she made bold decisions. She relocated, seeking a fresh start far from the reminders of who she once pretended to be. She took control of her finances, refusing to be financially dependent on anyone else.

Yet, the toughest step was redefining her relationships. She found her voice, set boundaries, and dared to disagree. Some friendships faded away, unable to accommodate her newfound assertiveness. And in her romantic life, she discovered her true value, refusing to settle for less than she deserved.

Recognizing that she needed support, she turned to therapy. It became her sanctuary—a place to unravel the complexities of her past and rebuild her sense of self-worth.

Shedding the label of good girl, she reclaimed her voice, her agency, and her authenticity. Now, she's neither good nor bad; she's simply Charlotte. And that's more than enough.

Eliza's Story

Raised in a strict catholic home, Eliza didn't have an opinion of her own. Forced into a belief system passed down from generations, she felt an internal struggle from a young age. She loved art and music, yet her mother would insist she study and "dress with respect."

She was the oldest daughter of three and was always told to set the example—to set the standard—for her sisters. She was a creative spirit with no outlet. She, like so many others, lost sight of her own dreams amid the pressures to fit into societal molds.

As she became an adult, she knew she needed to shine a light on who she really was and what she wanted out of life. Discovering the mechanisms of nice girl syndrome that kept her bound, she empowered herself to break free.

One of Eliza's key moments came when she ceased the relentless pursuit of people-pleasing. Saying *no* to others and *yes* to herself allowed her to claim her freedom and creativity and set healthy boundaries. No longer needing approval, she discovered the profound power of authenticity. She felt the growth.

Putting herself first was a radical act of self-love for Eliza. She refused to sacrifice her identity or compromise her true spirit to appease others. Rejecting the expectations of her family, she embraced her sense of self without shame or guilt, recognizing her desires as valid and worthy of expression.

Unlearning ingrained beliefs was no easy feat for Eliza. She confronted the notion that her elders and role models were infallible, realizing that their paths were not necessarily hers to follow. With each lesson unlearned, she grew stronger in her resolve to chart her own course.

Breaking free from the good girl mold was a freedom like no other for Eliza. Accepting her authenticity, she stepped into her power with newfound confidence and self-assurance. She hopes to inspire all women seeking to break free from societal constraints and embrace their true selves.

Conclusion: The Journey Ahead

We have concluded our exploration of *Breaking Up With Niceness*. This time of uncovering self-discovery and empowerment required significant courage and resolve, and your commitment to it is truly admirable. As we draw this journey to a close, I trust that you are not only enlightened but also emboldened, poised to embrace the principles of genuine self-care and assertiveness.

Throughout our time, we have meticulously dissected the complexities of nice girl syndrome, gaining insights into its manifestations and acknowledging its influence in our lives. You have bravely confronted ingrained patterns of people-pleasing behavior, reclaiming your autonomy and self-determination in the process. By reconceptualizing self-care as a fundamental act of prioritizing your own well-being, you have begun to foster a deeper sense of compassion and self-respect.

One of the most empowering revelations has been mastering the art of saying *no* and establishing boundaries that safeguard your time, energy, and emotional equilibrium. Through this process, you have reclaimed your voice, articulating your needs and preferences with confidence and conviction. Through introspection and the pursuit of authenticity, you have peeled away the layers of societal expectations, embracing your unique identity with conviction.

This is just the beginning of your commitment to personal growth and self-improvement. As you move forward, I urge you to continue to foster resilience and self-assurance, recognizing that setbacks are integral to growth. Accept each challenge as an opportunity for refinement and evolution, acknowledging the strides you have taken and the person you are becoming.

In conclusion, I offer a final message of empowerment: You are deserving of a life characterized by boldness and authenticity. Trust in your inherent strength and unwavering resolve, for genuine self-care is not a luxury but a fundamental right. Accept the freedom that comes from breaking free from the restraints of niceness, and move forward with confidence to a future illuminated by your own brilliance. I am confident that you will continue to flourish and thrive. Here's to embracing a life of boldness, authenticity, and unwavering self-respect.

About the Author

Sarah Barry is an author and Certified Professional Retirement and Life Transition Coach with over 35 years of experience spanning banking, fashion, events, and digital advertising. Born in Gibraltar, she has lived and worked across the UK, Australia, Japan, and Dubai in the UAE, where she is based today.

She spent much of that career being very good at putting others first. Accommodating, agreeable, endlessly available. It took her longer than she would like to admit to understand what that was costing her. That journey is what this book is built on.

Her writing explores the quieter side of how we lose ourselves, and how we find our way back. Through her books, coaching, and writing, she works with people navigating the kind of change that doesn't come with a clear roadmap.

She writes for the people who are done being endlessly accommodating, and ready to find out what they actually want. Her books and resources for what comes next are at sarahbarry.com.

JOIN OUR MAILING LIST

Scan the QR code below to sign up to our Newsletter mailing list and receive a free bonus gift.

Our newsletters are packed with valuable insights and actionable tips on self-care and personal growth. We're dedicated to providing quality content that's both empowering and practical, ensuring you receive inspiration without overwhelming your inbox with excessive emails.

Glossary

All definitions were sourced from Wiktionary.org.

Agency: Refers to the sense of control and autonomy individuals feel over their actions and decisions.

Aggressive communication: Expressing one's needs, feelings, or opinions in a forceful and confrontational manner, often disregarding the rights and feelings of others.

Assertiveness: Assertiveness refers to expressing one's needs, desires, opinions, and feelings in a direct and respectful manner, without infringing on the rights of others.

Assertive communication: Confidently expressing one's thoughts, feelings, and needs in a clear, respectful manner, while also considering the rights and perspectives of others.

Attachment theory: Early interactions between infants and caregivers shape lifelong patterns of behavior and relationships, influencing how individuals form emotional bonds and respond to intimacy throughout their lives.

Authenticity: Authenticity is the quality of being genuine, true to oneself, and aligned with one's values, beliefs, and emotions.

Boundaries: Boundaries are guidelines, rules, or limits that a person establishes to protect their physical, emotional, and mental well-being. Healthy boundaries define where one person ends and another begins.

Boldness: Boldness is the willingness to take risks, speak up, and assert oneself confidently, even in the face of uncertainty or opposition.

Calm under pressure: The ability to remain calm, composed, and resilient in challenging or stressful situations, maintaining integrity and poise.

Compassion: Compassion is the ability to understand and empathize with others' experiences, feelings, and suffering, coupled with a desire to alleviate it.

Confidence: Confidence is a belief in one's abilities, worth, and potential to succeed, thrive, and overcome challenges.

Conflict avoidance: The tendency to evade or minimize disagreements or confrontations, often at the expense of addressing underlying issues or maintaining authentic communication.

Conformity: The tendency of individuals to adjust their attitudes, beliefs, and behaviors to align with those of a group, often in response to social pressure or the desire for acceptance.

Dopamine: A neurotransmitter in the brain that plays a key role in regulating mood, motivation, reward processing, and movement.

Dysfunctional patterns: Dysfunctional patterns are recurring behaviors, thoughts, or beliefs that are detrimental to one's well-being and hinder personal growth and healthy relationships.

Emotional intelligence: Emotional intelligence is the ability to recognize, understand, and manage one's own emotions, as well as empathize with and influence the emotions of others.

Empowerment: Empowerment is the process of gaining control over one's life, making informed choices, and taking action to achieve personal goals and fulfillment.

External pressures: The influences, expectations, or demands exerted by factors outside of oneself, such as societal norms, cultural standards, or peer influences, which may impact individual behavior or decision-making.

Fear of consequences: Involves the apprehension or anxiety about potential negative outcomes or repercussions resulting from one's actions or decisions.

Fear of rejection: Fear of rejection is an irrational fear of being disapproved of, disliked, or abandoned by others, often leading individuals to avoid asserting their needs or setting boundaries.

Feminine strength: Feminine strength encompasses qualities traditionally associated with femininity, such as empathy, intuition, resilience, and nurturing, which are sources of power and influence.

Genuine self-care: Genuine self-care involves prioritizing one's physical, emotional, and mental well-being by engaging in activities and practices that nurture and replenish oneself.

Healthy relationships: Healthy relationships are characterized by mutual respect, trust, communication, support, and the ability to maintain individual identities while fostering connection.

Independence: Independence is the ability to rely on oneself, make autonomous decisions, and take responsibility for one's actions, choices, and well-being.

Inner strength: Inner strength refers to the resilience, courage, and fortitude that enable individuals to navigate challenges, setbacks, and adversity with grace and determination.

Integrity: Integrity is the quality of being honest, ethical, and consistent in one's actions, values, and principles, even when faced with challenges or temptations.

Internal pressures: The personal beliefs, values, desires, or expectations that individuals experience within themselves, influencing their thoughts, emotions, and behaviors.

Interpersonal dynamics: The complex interactions and relationships between individuals, encompassing communication patterns, power dynamics, emotional exchanges, and social behaviors within social contexts.

Justice: Justice is the principle of fairness, equity, and moral righteousness, advocating for equality, rights, and dignity for oneself and others.

Limiting beliefs: Limiting beliefs are negative or self-sabotaging thoughts and beliefs that undermine one's self-confidence, potential, and ability to achieve goals.

Mental resilience: Mental resilience is the ability to bounce back from adversity, setbacks, and challenges, maintaining clarity, adaptability, and optimism in the face of difficulties.

Mindfulness: Mindfulness is the practice of cultivating present-moment awareness, non-judgmentally observing thoughts, feelings, sensations, and the environment.

Mirror neurons: A type of brain cell that activates both when an individual performs an action and when they observe the same action being performed by another, facilitating empathy, imitation, and understanding of others' behaviors and intentions.

Nice girl syndrome: Nice girl syndrome refers to a behavioral pattern characterized by excessive people-pleasing, avoidance of conflict, and prioritizing others' needs over one's own at the expense of personal well-being.

Nonviolent communication: Nonviolent communication is a method of interpersonal communication focused on expressing oneself honestly and empathically, while also listening with empathy and resolving conflicts peacefully.

Openness: Openness is a willingness to embrace new experiences, ideas, perspectives, and opportunities, fostering growth, learning, and connection.

Optimism: Optimism is a positive outlook on life characterized by hope, confidence, and resilience, even in the face of challenges, setbacks, and uncertainty.

Passive communication: Involves a reluctance to express one's own thoughts, feelings, or needs, often leading to a lack of assertiveness, passive-aggressive behavior, and unaddressed grievances.

People-pleasing: People-pleasing is a tendency to prioritize others' needs, desires, and opinions over one's own, often at the expense of personal boundaries, values, and well-being.

Perception of assertiveness: The subjective evaluation of how confidently and respectfully one communicates their thoughts, feelings, and needs while considering the perspectives and boundaries of others.

Personal growth: Personal growth is the ongoing process of self-improvement, learning, and development, encompassing emotional, psychological, and spiritual evolution.

Resilience: Resilience is the ability to adapt, bounce back, and thrive in the face of adversity, setbacks, and challenges.

Self-care: Self-care is the practice of prioritizing one's physical, emotional, and mental well-being through activities, habits, and rituals that promote relaxation, rejuvenation, and nourishment.

Self-compassion: Self-compassion involves treating oneself with kindness, understanding, and acceptance, especially during times of struggle, failure, or suffering.

Self-doubt: Self-doubt is a lack of confidence or belief in one's abilities, worth, or potential, often leading to hesitation, indecision, and avoidance of risks or opportunities.

Self-reflection: Self-reflection is the process of introspection and examination of one's thoughts, emotions, behaviors, and experiences, facilitating self-awareness, growth, and learning.

Societal reinforcement: The process by which cultural norms, expectations, and institutions uphold and perpetuate certain behaviors, values, and beliefs through socialization, rewards, and sanctions.

Toxic relationships: Toxic relationships are characterized by negativity, manipulation, emotional abuse, and lack of respect, often detrimental to one's self-esteem and well-being.

Trust: Trust is the foundation of healthy relationships, built on reliability, honesty, transparency, and mutual respect, fostering intimacy, connection, and security.

Unconditional self-worth: Unconditional self-worth is the inherent belief in one's inherent value and deservingness, irrespective of external achievements, validation

Victim mentality: Victim mentality is a mindset characterized by a belief that one is powerless, helpless, or unfairly treated by circumstances or others, often leading to passivity and self-pity.

Wellness practices: Wellness practices encompass a range of activities, habits, and rituals aimed at promoting physical, emotional, and mental well-being, such as exercise, meditation, and self-care routines.

References

Ackerman, C. E. (2017, December 21). *9 self-compassion exercises & worksheets (+ PDF)*. PositivePsychology.com. https://positivepsychology.com/self-compassion-exercises-worksheets/

Adams, B. T. (2023, April 26). *Fearless forward: Overcoming obstacles and conquering fears for personal and professional growth*. LinkedIn. https://www.linkedin.com/pulse/fearless-forward-overcoming-obstacles-conquering-fears-adams/

Alexander, K. L. (n.d.). *Florence Nightingale*. National Women's History Museum. https://www.womenshistory.org/education-resources/biographies/florence-nightingale

Ballard, J. (2022, August 22). *Women are more likely than men to say they're a people-pleaser, and many dislike being seen as one*. YouGov. https://today.yougov.com/society/articles/43498-women-more-likely-men-people-pleasing-poll

Beecham, A. (2023, June). *The 8 types of boundaries you should be setting at work, in relationships and with friends*. Stylist. https://www.stylist.co.uk/relationships/types-of-boundaries/683749

Bii, E. (2023, November 4). *Boundaries 101: Practicing assertive communication for setting and communicating boundaries*. Medium. https://toxicrelationships.medium.com/boundaries-101-

practicing-assertive-communication-for-setting-and-communicating-boundaries-d8e6e5b6762c

Blackstone, A. M. (2003). *Gender roles and society*. [Sociology School Faculty Scholarship, University of Maine]. DigitalCommons@UMaine. https://digitalcommons.library.umaine.edu/soc_facpub/1/

Bowen, L. (2018, February 16). *Getting over my good girl syndrome*. Ravishly. https://www.ravishly.com/getting-over-my-good-girl-syndrome

Carey, T. (2018, July 17). *Why are yawns contagious? We asked a scientist*. PBS NewsHour. https://www.pbs.org/newshour/science/why-are-yawns-contagious-we-asked-a-scientist

Cikanavicius, D. (2017, August 28). The trap of external validation for self-esteem. *Psych Central*. https://psychcentral.com/blog/psychology-self/2017/08/validation-self-esteem

Damon, C. (n.d.). 7 effective goal setting techniques. *AchieveIt*. https://www.achieveit.com/resources/blog/7-effective-goal-setting-techniques/

Dhabhar, F. S. (2014). Effects of stress on immune function: The good, the bad, and the beautiful. *Immunologic Research, 58*, 193–210. https://doi.org/10.1007/s12026-014-8517-0

Embracing resilience: Developing a growth mindset. (2023, November 27). Center for Health & Well-Being. https://www.ie.edu/center-for-health-and-well-being/blog/embracing-resilience-developing-a-growth-mindset/

Erden, F., & Wolfgang, C. (2004). An exploration of the differences in prekindergarten, kindergarten, and first grade teachers' beliefs related to discipline when dealing with male and female

students. *Early Child Development and Care, 174*(1), 3–11.
https://psycnet.apa.org/record/2004-11507-001

Gatchpazian, A. (n.d.). *Assertive communication: Definition, examples, &*
techniques. The Berkeley Well-Being Institute.
https://www.berkeleywellbeing.com/assertive-
communication.html

Gattuso, R. (2018, August 9). *How does people pleasing negatively affect your*
mental health? Talkspace.
https://www.talkspace.com/blog/people-pleasing-negatively-
affect-mental-health/

GGI Insights. (2024, May 21). *Gender roles: Navigating the dynamics of*
societal expectations. Gray Group International.
https://www.graygroupintl.com/blog/gender-roles

Glowiak, M. (2024, January 23). *What is self-care and why is it important for*
you? Southern New Hampshire University.
https://www.snhu.edu/about-us/newsroom/health/what-is-
self-care

Hullett, A. (2023, April 5). *50 shades of self-Care: How to give yourself TLC*
for every occasion. Greatist. https://greatist.com/health/types-of-
self-care

Huntington, C. (n.d.). *People pleasing: Definition, quotes, & psychology.* The
Berkeley Well-Being Institute.
https://www.berkeleywellbeing.com/people-pleasing.html

Indian Girl Gone Rogue. (2024, February 29). *The nice girl syndrome.*
Medium. https://iggr.medium.com/the-nice-girl-syndrome-
6fb5927950f6

Jen. (2023, March 22). How to stop seeking external validation. *The*
Meaningful Bits of Life Blog.
https://meaningfulbitsoflife.com/2023/02/02/stop-seeking-
external-validation/

Kelly B. (2023, February 13). *Top 5 reasons to stop seeking validation & how to spot it*. LinkedIn. https://www.linkedin.com/pulse/top-5-reasons-stop-seeking-validation-how-spot-kelly-blackmon/

Mahrer, B. (2019, December 16). *Why you struggle with self-care*. NAMI. https://www.nami.org/stress-management/why-you-struggle-with-self-care/

Martinez, N., Connelly, C. D., Pérez, A., & Calero, P. (2021). Self-care: A concept analysis. *International Journal of Nursing Sciences, 8*(4), 418-425. https://doi.org/10.1016/j.ijnss.2021.08.007

Matthews, P. (2023, October 17). *Understanding the connection between people pleasing, early childhood trauma, and autoimmune response*. LinkedIn. https://www.linkedin.com/pulse/understanding-connection-between-people-pleasing-early-paul-matthews/

Papayanis, A. (2022, January 7). *Women are taught to be nice. Here's what happened when I stopped*. HuffPost. https://www.huffpost.com/entry/women-socialized-to-be-nice_n_61d7612be4b04b42ab7d7196

Patel, A. (2023, June 10). *Healthy boundaries vs. unhealthy boundaries*. Arati Patel, LMFT. https://www.aratipatel.com/boundaries/understanding-healthy-and-unhealthy-boundaries/

Pipas, M. D., & Jaradat, M. (2010). Assertive communication skills. *Fundamental Studies of Economic Research Journal, 12*(2), 649–656. https://www.researchgate.net/publication/227367804_Assertive_Communication_Skills

Stories From Tina. (2024, January 17). *Shaking off the nice girl syndrome: The power of setting boundaries*. Medium. https://medium.com/@chinyereokoli/shaking-off-the-nice-girl-syndrome-the-power-of-setting-boundaries-777a48c49f29

Strong, R. (2024, February 1). *Toxic femininity, explained—Plus, tips to overcome this mindset*. Healthline.

https://www.healthline.com/health/mental-health/toxic-femininity#definition-andexamples

Suttie, J. (2013, December 2). Why are we so wired to connect? *Greater Good.* https://greatergood.berkeley.edu/article/item/why_are_we_so _wired_to_connect

Sutton, A. (2020). Living the good life: A meta-analysis of authenticity, well-being and engagement. *Personality and Individual Differences, 153*(6). https://doi.org/10.1016/j.paid.2019.109645

Tips for increasing assertive communication. (n.d.). St. Joseph's Healthcare Hamilton. https://www.stjoes.ca/our-stories/news/~1890-Tips-for-increasing-assertive-communication

Vanourek, G. (2023, July 20). *Setting boundaries—Why it's hard and how to do it.* LinkedIn. https://www.linkedin.com/pulse/setting-boundarieswhy-its-hard-how-do-gregg-vanourek/

Varghese, S. (2023, September 10). *How I overcame good girl syndrome!* LinkedIn. https://www.linkedin.com/pulse/how-i-overcame-good-girl-syndrome-salini-varghese/

Wiktionary. (n.d.). *Wiktionary, the free encyclopedia.* Wiktionary.org. Retrieved May 30, 2024 https://en.wiktionary.org/wiki/Wiktionary:Main_Page

Yegorov, Y. E., Poznyak, A. V., Nikiforov, N. G., Sobenin, I. A., & Orekhov, A. N. (2020). The link between chronic stress and accelerated aging. *Biomedicines, 8*(7), 198. https://doi.org/10.3390/biomedicines8070198